MASTERING YOUR INTUITION

How To Get Answers From God And Your Soul

BY ALLIE DUZETT

Other books by Allie Duzett:

Deep Past Resolution: Empower Your Future
By Resolving Your Pre-Earth Past

The Scribbling Solution: A Simple, Revolutionary Way to Release
the Energies Affecting Weight, Health, Relationships, Abundance,
and More

Heal Your Ancestors, Heal Yourself: Easily Heal Ancestral and
Generational Trauma

30 Days of Belief Work Series

30 Days of Belief Work: The Jumpstart

30 Days of Belief Work: Boundaries

30 Days of Belief Work: Finances

30 Days of Belief Work: Sleep

30 Days of Belief Work: Hormones

All books available on Amazon

Join me on Facebook: Intuitive Healing With Allie Duzett

Table of Contents

Chapter 1: Introduction 1

    The Structure Of This Book 6

Chapter 2: Becoming Inspired 8

    Intuitive Calibration Instructions 11

    When Intuitive Calibration Doesn't Work.............................. 14

    How People Become Shallow Breathers............................... 15

    Benefits of Deeper Breathing.. 19

    Conclusion 23

Chapter 3: Experiencing Pranayam 24

    Long, Slow, Deep Breathing.. 25

    Single Nostril Breathing.. 25

    Alternate Nostril Breathing 26

    Breath of Fire 26

    Conclusion 27

Chapter 4: The Beliefs That Frame Your Experience........... 28

    Assess Your Experience.. 33

    Creating Your Own Tapping Scripts....................................... 34

    Conclusion 35

Chapter 5: Your Body Is The Vessel 36

    The Nervous System and Emotional Health 38

Toxicity and the Nervous System.................................41

Nutrition and the Nervous System 43

Conclusion...54

Chapter 6: Strengthening the Nervous System........55

Yoga for the Nervous System..................................56

Humming and Singing...60

Gargling...60

Other Nerve Strengthening Exercises 61

Shaking It Out 62

Cold Showers 63

Additional Nerve Strengthening Activities 64

Conclusion...65

Chapter 7: Harnessing the Conductor 66

The Electrical Nature of Spirits...............................67

Water as the Conductor 71

Rules for Getting Hydrated 73

Electrolyte Needs 75

Hydration for Spiritual Connection...........................76

A Note About Types of Water 77

Conclusion...79

Chapter 8: Accessing the Divine Polarity..................80

The Prerequisites to Spiritual Awakening.....................82

My Repentance Process...84

Living in Alignment With Spiritual Blueprints.................88

Gendered Spirituality 90

A Brief Introduction to the Polarity 93

The Polarity Is Relative 96

Stepping into Healthy Expressions of Spiritual Biology 98

Intuition and Your Marriage 105

Conclusion 115

Chapter 9: Alignment, Body and Spirit 116

Getting Your Spiritual Side In Order 119

Making Restitution 122

Heartfelt Apologies 122

When You Can't Apologize 126

Financial Restitution 128

Tithing 131

Trauma and Mistakes 132

When Things Cannot Be Fixed 133

The Forgiveness List 134

How to Forgive 135

The Third List: Your Trauma and Victimhood 140

The Bonus List 142

Conclusion 143

Chapter 10: Four Keys to Success 144

Grounding 145

Polarity 149

Calling Back Your Personal Power 150

You Deserve The Answers You Seek 154

Conclusion 156

Chapter 11: Beginning to Receive......................................**157**

When You're Not Used to Receiving Answers.................... 158

Everyone is Different 159

What About Empaths?.. 161

Beginning to Receive 162

Conclusion... 165

Chapter 12: Asking the Right Questions...................**166**

Backing Up For Better Answers............................. 169

The Power of Yes-No Questions............................. 171

Taking Action... 172

Double Checking.. 173

Conclusion... 174

Chapter 13: Healing Intuition Trauma **175**

Scribbling Out Intuition Trauma 175

Scribbling Prompts... 179

Healing Pre-Earth Trauma Around Intuition.......... 184

Guided Imagery: Tube of Light............................. 186

Additional Tapping Scripts 187

Chapter 14: The School of Trust.............................**189**

Setting the Parameters 192

Going Back To School 193

The School of Trust.. 194

Involving Other People 195

Asking For the Unmistakable and Obvious............. 197

Conclusion... 198

Chapter 15: The Power of Writing For Powerful Insight ... 200

Journaling for Spiritual Insight 201

Troubleshooting Journaling For Spiritual Guidance 203

Scribbling for Emotional Clearing 207

Analyzing Your Scribbles 213

Prayer Journaling Challenge 215

Tapping Scripts for Successful Prayer Journaling 216

Ideas for Prayer Journaling Topics........................... 217

Conclusion 219

Chapter 16: A Life-Changing Self-Healing Exercise 220

Using This Technique For Receiving Answers..................... 223

Opening to Healing When You Struggle to Be Open 224

When the Self-Healing Exercise Is Really Intense 226

Conclusion 227

Chapter 17: When There Is No Answer................................ 228

Stop Me If It's Wrong.. 229

Think About It Tomorrow....................................... 230

Drawing From An Empty Well................................. 231

Praying for a Stepping Stone.................................. 232

Rest in Peace 233

Conclusion 235

Chapter 18: A Final Note 236

Chapter 1

Introduction

Life is hard when you can't hear the voice of God, or the voice of your own inner wisdom! All of us deal with situations where we yearn for divine guidance, but many of us struggle to hear that voice of the divine when we need it most. We ask the questions that weigh on our souls—but what happens when there is no answer?

What happens when we feel that it's impossible to receive divine wisdom about our personal lives?

I often hear from beloved friends, students, and clients who are struggling because they don't feel like they are getting the answers to the questions they are aching for answers to. Sometimes the problem is that they don't feel like they can trust the answers they receive; sometimes they feel they aren't getting any answers at all.

When we struggle to receive trustworthy answers to the questions we have about our lives, it can lead to feelings of despair, and of divine indifference. "God and the Universe itself must not care about me. I must not be important." These are the kinds of thoughts we can think when we feel divinely ignored, and these are not exactly empowering, joyful thoughts.

The purpose of this book is specifically to help people who feel divinely ignored. Is this you?

Do you feel like you struggle to receive answers to the questions you have about your life? Are you a praying person, but you never feel like you get answers to your prayers? Or maybe you are not a praying person, but still feel like you never have the clear intuitive insight on the big decisions of your life? Do you get answers occasionally, but feel like you can't trust them completely?

Feeling divinely led through our lives adds such a huge layer of comfort and peace to even our difficult experiences; feeling divinely ignored can lead to feelings of confusion and even depression.

I believe we can shift out of this space of feeling divinely ignored. As we build the "muscles" necessary to recognize divine and intuitive guidance as it shows up, we can get better and better at this skill.

Yes: I called it a skill. I do believe that our Higher Power is never ignoring us. When we ask a question of our Divine Source, our Source ALWAYS answers us. Whether or not we are ready to hear the answer, or skilled enough to recognize the answer, we are getting an answer. I truly believe this. I truly believe that all of us are practically swimming in a sea of spiritual information that is fully available to us—if only we would develop the skills necessary to recognize, harness, and act on this information.

This book is about doing what it takes to perceive, recognize, and act on spiritual information. The sources of spiritual information that matter most to me are what I call divine guidance, and intuition.

What is the difference?

To me, divine guidance comes from our Source. I call Him God. But if you are not a believer in God, or some other divine entity, I refer to this miraculous life-giving energy as our Source, our Creator, or the Divine. To me, divine guidance comes from a loving, omniscient, omnipotent energy that loves *you* and wants *you specifically* to be happy and live an incredible and blessed life.

Intuition is different because it comes from within us. Where guidance from our Source comes from our Source, intuition comes from the Higher Self. When I talk about the Higher Self, I am referring to the part of the human spirit that exists beyond time: the part of the human spirit that has already lived this human life and now is full of wisdom for us to draw upon.

If our spirits are eternal, and I believe they are, this means they exist both inside and outside of Time. We are experiencing mortal life embodied on the Earth at this time, but at the same time, we are also existing outside of time. I believe there is a part of each person's spirit that has already "been there, done that," due to the nature of time, spirits, and eternity. When we draw on our own intuition, we are tapping into that energy, wisdom, and knowledge.

For me, I personally am a Christian, although you do not have to be a Christian in order to get a lot out of this book. But to explain the relationship between intuition and divine guidance from a Christian perspective, you can think of it like this. In the Christian theology, or at least some Christian theologies, we all live on this Earth and then eventually die, and because of Christ's atonement we will be resurrected and live eternally. Eternity is outside of time. Somewhere in existence, considering Time as one great whole, we have already gone through our Earth lives and been judged and experienced resurrection—on some level, all of us have already done this and now live beyond Time in eternity.

When we tune into our own intuition, this is the part of ourselves I believe we are accessing. To me, the relationship between personal intuition and divine guidance can be compared to the relationship between God and Jesus Christ. I believe God and Christ are separate in Their way, but united in message, purpose, and intention. Jesus taught in the Holy Bible to pray to God, not to Jesus. To me, this is similar to the relationship between our internal intuition and divine guidance. Divine guidance comes from God, or our Creator or

Source. Intuition comes from within. But both divine guidance and intuition share the same purpose and mission and intention, just like God and Jesus are different but share the same purpose and mission. At the same time, to me, we prioritize divine guidance over intuition just like Jesus taught in the Holy Bible to prioritize the relationship with God even over the relationship with Jesus. Both relationships are critical and important and life-changing, but one does take some amount of precedence over the other.

In my experience and observation, intuition and divine guidance are typically united in purpose and message, and listening to either of them is a good choice, especially since they will typically lead to the same actions. But I do recognize the distinction between them. For myself, if there's ever a conflict between what I feel like I want and what I feel the Divine wants, which has on rare occasions happened, I opt to follow what I feel the Divine is telling me to do.

One more aspect of intuition relates to the body. This is the concept that our physical bodies contain wisdom for us that is important to know. This is the wisdom that comes from being embodied. What I am talking about is the wisdom from your body that knows if you need more sleep, or more amino acids, or more fun in order to be happy and healthy. I believe our physical bodies are also repositories of wisdom and when we tune into our physical bodies, we are accessing a different sort of intuition as well. This intuition is also important and worth considering. We'll talk about it more throughout the book.

But to recap, the goal of this book is to gain a better relationship with our ability to receive guidance from the Divine, from our own intuition, and even from our own physical bodies. Typically these sources of information will agree, because they are united in purpose: they want us to live the best life we can. They want us to be happy and healthy.

The Structure Of This Book

You'll notice that this book covers a wide variety of material, and I put it in a particular order. I did that on purpose. I know many people want to jump right into intuitive exercises and so on, and I beg you not to.

I know that many people feel their big problem is just that they can't quiet their brain well enough to listen clearly to divine guidance.

No matter where you feel your own problems originate, I hope you will read this book in order. Many times in life, the struggles we experience have their root in trying to skip steps. This is what I hope to avoid with the structure of this book. We start at the very beginning, with the most foundational aspect of receiving divine answers: getting our physical bodies in order.

From there, we begin to get our minds and spirits in order.

Then we heal some of our intuition-related trauma and learn how to ask the right questions. We practice asking and listening for answers. We learn how to discern for ourselves the answers that we receive.

All these things go hand in hand but it's important to address the physical body first. So you will appreciate reading this book in order and gaining what you can from each chapter in the order in which it was written. It would be sad to skip ahead and do intuitive exercises from the end, and then have them fail you because you missed out on critical information from Chapter 2!

Keep breathing and keep reading! We're going to work together to develop some new skills to clearly understand divine guidance, intuitive guidance, and even body guidance, and this journey may very well change your life.

Chapter 2

Becoming Inspired

Sometimes when people talk about receiving divine guidance or spiritual information, they call it "inspiration." I think this is an incredibly perfect word for it! The word "inspire" comes from the Latin *inspirare*, "to breathe." This is the root word of "respiration" as well as "inspiration." When it comes to feeling inspired—or in other words, divinely led and guided—**breath** must be a primary concern.

Consider Genesis 2:7, from the Holy Bible: "And the Lord God formed man of the dust of the ground, and breathed into his nostrils the breath of life; and man became a living soul."

When God created man, He made man's body and put man's spirit inside. But until Adam breathed the breath of life, he was not considered a "living soul." Biblically speaking, breath is what unites a body and a spirit.

Dharma Singh Khalsa, MD once wrote, "Breath is life, and life is but a series of breaths." Indeed, the ancients understood that life and breath and spirit are all just aspects of the same thing. The Greek word *pneuma* means both "soul" and "breath." The Latin *anima spiritus* means both "spirit" and "breath." The Hebrew word for breath is the same exact word as is used for "Spirit of God." To "inspire" literally means to "breathe in," so there may be some application to the idea that if you are having trouble feeling divine guidance, maybe you need to breathe more deeply to get inspired. There is an ancient understanding that the spirit and the breath are uniquely, deeply connected.

The breath is miraculous because it is one of two automatic bodily processes that can be controlled by the conscious mind—the other, incidentally, is blinking, which is also rich in symbolism and in application. Because of this unique aspect of breath, being a process that is both conscious and subconscious, we can actually use the breath to access the subconscious mind.

Understanding the subconscious mind is deeply important to living in alignment with the Divine. How many of us have had an experience where, in the moment we knew what we were doing was wrong, but it just came to us so second-nature that we couldn't stop it? Those moments are run by the subconscious mind. And even though we may not have felt in control of ourselves in those moments, the things we do and the bad choices we make under the influence of the subconscious mind are still things we need to repent of. How much better, though, to go to the source of the issue and make the changes there! Using breath and Kundalini Yoga, we have the opportunity to reach into the inner recesses of our subconscious mind, and begin letting go of the patterns and beliefs that lead us to sin.

Yogi Bhajan, the first teacher of Kundalini Yoga in the West, taught that most people breathe too shallowly to maintain even normal health. So as you focus on your breathing this week and in the future, you will notice a shift in both your physical and mental health.

In Kundalini Yoga, one of the most important aspects of the breath is called *prana*. Prana basically refers to the life force--what Asians call *chi* and what quantum physicists call *zero point energy* and what the Christian scriptures call *the light of Christ*, the energy that is in all things and powers all things (see Doctrine and Covenants 88:6-13). What a singer might call "breath control" is a way to harness and access the power of prana to energize the body for maximum physical and spiritual health.

And what a singer might call "breath control" may also be key to feeling "inspired." Because, remember, the word "inspire" literally means "to breathe in." When we struggle to feel inspired, it is time to breathe in!

I wanted to get this book started with some very practical techniques that you could use immediately. One of the most important things you can do is learn to breathe sufficiently for normal health. You will find that as you breathe more deeply more regularly, you will experience massive positive shifts in every area of your life, but especially in the area of receiving divine guidance.

In the Free Offerings of my website, allieduzettclasses.com, I have a free class called Intuitive Calibration. In this class, students learn to use the power of their breath to discern divine answers. For those that aren't familiar with the technique, these are the instructions.

Intuitive Calibration Instructions

You start your own intuitive calibration by taking deep breaths and closing your eyes. After a few deep breaths, you ask your body: "Body, what does a 'yes' feel like?" And you just breathe and breathe and see what it feels like in your body. **Please note that if you are a chronic shallow breather, it may take some weeks of consistent deeper breathing to get to the point where your body is prepared to feel very different when you do this exercise**. This exercise can be very effective, but if you are a habitual shallow breather, you may need to spend some weeks building up your breathing power and really practicing this exercise.

When I asked one class of students to describe how they felt when asking their bodies to show them a "yes" feeling, this is what they came up with:

- feelings of spiritual expansion
- feelings of energy rising in the body
- feelings of spiritual "smiling"open feelings in the heart area
- feelings of light or warmth or tingling in the lungs and face

After you spend a few minutes feeling what a "yes" feels like in *your* body, shake yourself out literally by shaking your hands and feet and wiggling around a bit, and try again. This time, though, ask: "Body, what does a 'no' feel like?" And breathe and breathe again, so deeply, and see what a "no" feels like in your body. Remember that if you are a habitual shallow breather, it will be worth your time to build up your ability to breathe more deeply when trying to take advantage of this exercise.

When I asked that same group of students to describe a "no" feeling, they came up with this list:

- feelings of being closed off
- energy sinking downward instead of upward
- tingling on different parts of the body (one person's guts sometimes tingle when their body is telling them no, and another person's ears tingle)
- feelings of constriction

With this process of intuitive calibration, you can have a baseline for understanding how your own body communicates with you, and if your body is trying to give you a "false yes" or a "false no," you will also know how to spot that. You could also ask your body to show you how it feels when your body is trying to confuse you.

In case you are wondering why a body might try to confuse its owner, sometimes our bodies or subconscious minds try to confuse our conscious selves because they think it will keep us safe. The primary function of both the body and the subconscious mind is to keep us as safe as possible. Sometimes new concepts make the subconscious mind uncomfortable because they may prompt changes that seem unsafe. If or when this happens, the subconscious mind can respond to these concepts with confusion designed to prevent us from making changes that seem scary.

But when you put in the time and work to truly get acquainted with your body's responses to "yes" and "no," it can simplify your life enormously.

If you are a praying person, you can use this technique in combination with prayer. You do this by asking in prayer for God to show you through your own body's feelings and sensations how He communicates with you the ideas of "yes" and "no" (and "maybe"--which is sometimes an answer as well!).

If you are not a praying person, you can use this as an easy way to immediately discern your own soul's feelings about a situation, right there, in the moment.

Either way, this is a simple but profound technique for getting more in tune with your own self and living more fully in a space of true integrity to your own soul.

I urge you to try this technique before reading any further. One beautiful thing about life *is* that it is a series of breaths, which means that once you master this technique, you can feel it instantly any time anything *is* in alignment with you, or if it isn't.

This technique has been enormously powerful for me and for many of my clients and students—but still some people struggle with it. There are a few possible reasons why this can happen, and we're going to go through them.

When Intuitive Calibration Doesn't Work

When intuitive calibration doesn't work, it can come down to a number of things and we're going to explore and troubleshoot each one in this book. But this list of reasons can include:

- a history of habitual shallow breathing
- nervous system damage
- cellular malnutrition

- subconscious belief programming
- interference from negative energies

Before we move on to any other thing, right here in this chapter I want to guide you through some breathing exercises. As you go through this book, always remember that if your breathing is shallow, that is your first and most important problem to address.

How People Become Shallow Breathers

Shallow breathing is the natural response to stress. Go ahead and think back to the last time you had a big stressful event in your life. Maybe it was a big thing, like the death of a loved one, or maybe it was something less drastic. In my case, I'm distinctly remembering last night, when I took four of my five little kids to the symphony for the first time—solo. I wasn't planning to bring my three-year-old, but she demanded to come and I had ordered a ticket for my husband before we realized he had an important meeting online at the same time. So when my little daughter marched out to the car on our way out the door, I allowed her to come and use the extra ticket instead of staying home with Dad.

But actually it turns out there are really great reasons not to bring a three-year-old to the symphony. The show began at 7:30 PM, and her bedtime is 7:45 PM, for one thing. We got there early and those fifteen minutes of "nothing happening" left my little girl in distress. I ended up holding her on my lap during the entire performance, begging her to be quiet while she ignored me.

Fortunately, this was a 45-minute performance designed for little kids and she was hardly the only disruptive child in the audience, but it was still a stressful event for me! And in those moments where my child was complaining that she wanted to go home *right now*, my default response was... to stop breathing.

At this point in my life I know better, and when my body starts shutting down on me like that, I remind it that we don't get to just stop breathing every time we feel stressed. So I noticed myself turning to breathlessness as a response and consciously chose into deeper breathing instead.When stress crops up, it's time to *start* breathing, not stop!

But think back to your most recent stressful event—and prime your mind to pay attention during your next stressful event. Because I will bet most readers don't make it through the next twenty-four hours without some kind of stressful event showing up that affects your breathing patterns.

Think back to that last stressful moment, and think back to how it made you feel in your chest and lungs. Remember the tightness of it.

When we are stressed, most people just stop breathing. We start to hold our breath and when we do breathe again, it is irregular and shallow, *and this is normal*. It is normal to do this. This is normal, but it isn't ideal. And even though this can be a normal response to stress, over time, it compounds and can become a very big problem.

This is because most people experience stressful events fairly regularly, but most people also don't know how to fully remove those stressful events from their system.

Take yourself as a prime example. I want you to think of a time you felt embarrassed or humiliated. Can you think of that time? And think of how your body felt during that experience?

And now—ask yourself. When you think about that experience now, do you feel neutral and calm? Can you easily laugh it off because it was in the past and no longer matters?

Or do you still feel the weight of it in your chest? When you think of being embarrassed or humiliated like that, does your breath still catch in your chest? Do you still feel yourself recoiling with stress and regret?

Hopefully for you personally, my dear reader, you can laugh about that moment of embarrassment, whatever it was. But I will let you in on a secret: most readers are *not* anywhere close to releasing those moments of past embarrassment. For many people in this world, their past moments of humiliation are practically seared into their bodies, and on some level, their breath still reflects this.

And it's not just embarrassment and humiliation. Virtually any negative emotion can lead to breathing irregularity, and the longer we go without resolving those emotions, the longer our breathing irregularities continue.

One great example of this is betrayal trauma. Have you ever been betrayed by a loved one you deeply trusted? I actually have. And when that person came and confessed to me the truth, even though my brain went into a place of calm and forgiveness, my physical body did not. Instead, my physical body went into shock for weeks. I lost twelve pounds in two weeks because my body refused to eat. And I struggled to breathe normally because my body was stuck in this space of trauma.

Many, many people have been betrayed. I would guess that all humans have been betrayed, at one point or another. We experience heart-rending betrayal at the hands of friends, siblings, parents, teachers and authority figures, spouses, and more. And every time we experience a betrayal that leaves us reeling, our physical bodies bear the brunt of it and it all affects our breathing.

So when it comes to breath irregularity and shallow breathing, our emotional health can have a lot to do with it. Many people who do healing work as found in allieduzettclasses.com report that their breathing deepens and feels "freer" after clearing emotional trauma. However, this is a two-way street.

Earlier I mentioned that the breath is one natural conduit to the subconscious mind. This is because we breathe whether we want to or not: our subconscious mind manages that for us. But we can also control our breath consciously. What this means is that we can use our breath as a bridge.

What this means is that if we struggle to clear our emotions, and therefore have a hard time breathing more deeply, instead we can circumvent that process and go backwards: experience emotional healing by focusing on deepening the breath.

Any breathwork we do strengthens our entire body. Deeper breathing oxygenates our lungs, blood, brain, muscles, nerves; deeper breathing gives us greater sensitivity to the changes present in our body when we do exercises like intuitive calibration. So breathwork needs to be a top priority when we are seeking divine guidance—especially when we are seeking divine guidance about health.

Benefits of Deeper Breathing

There are TONS of benefits to breathing more deeply. These are just a few of them.

Your lymphatic system depends on you getting enough oxygen. Your heart pumps your blood, but your BREATH pumps your lymph. Your lymph system is part of your immune system and helps you stay healthy in times of distress. It also helps your body detox. Lymph cleans up and moderates the fluid in your body; if you have any kind of chronic swelling, that can have to do with stagnant lymph. And stagnant lymph comes back to the breath. Again: while your heart pumps your blood, your breath pumps your lymph. If you want to improve your immune system function and reduce your overall inflammation, improve your breathing.

Some places claim that 70% of our body's detox processes are supposed to be completed through breathing: the body is supposed to expel 70% of its toxic material through the breath. The lungs are an incredible detox organ *if* we use them correctly. Chronically breathing shallowly does not take advantage of the incredible power of the lungs to help us expel toxic material from our bodies.

And speaking of expelling toxic material, carbon dioxide is toxic to us! We have to expel it! Having high levels of carbon dioxide in the body can lead to headaches, fatigue, blood pressure problems, restlessness, dizziness, and brain fog (among other things). If you deal with any of those symptoms, it's possible that just breathing more deeply could help you manage those symptoms significantly.

Deep breathing improves posture. To actually breathe deeply enough for a breath to be considered a "deep" breath, you can't really be slumped over. When your attention turns to your breath, better posture is a natural side effect because to breathe appropriately your posture must shift as well. This is important because good posture is necessary for proper blood flow and proper energy flow. Good posture is also important for our bones. We reduce our physical and even emotional stress in life when we have better posture, and we can achieve better posture through that primary goal of just breathing more deeply.

Deep breathing releases pain. Have you experienced this? As a mother, this is the first thing I pull out of my mental first aid kit any time a child comes to me with physical pain. "Take some deep breaths!" I guide them through the breathing process and they calm down. I've had three unmedicated home births, and the pain was very manageable with deep breathing (and mental training). Most people shut down their breathing and start holding their breath when something hurts, but choosing into deep breaths can help moderate and reduce the pain.

Breathing more deeply strengthens the lungs and other key organs. Organs are muscles in their own way—they literally are made of up muscle tissue along with the other parts of them. But breathing more deeply can actually exercise and strengthen and tone our lungs and other important organs. Think of it like exercise for your internal organs.

Deep breathing helps clean our blood as it floods us with oxygen and removes toxic waste. Having more oxygen means the body works more efficiently.

Breathing more deeply leads to better sleep and more relaxation. Deep breathing soothes the nervous system as well, which is one reason why we really want to breathe more deeply.

Shortness of breath is significantly linked to depression and can be a leading indicator of depression—so healing the breath can help heal depression as well. Deep breathing supports proper brain health, because there is a huge link between the respiratory system and neurochemistry.

AND you can use breath FOR HEALING energetically as well as physically. In my class called You Are a Healer, on allieduzettclasses.com, I teach how to use the breath to heal your physical body and your emotions.

I hope all of this information has led you to conclude one thing: that changing how you breathe may change your life.

On a religious level, it has been noted that the Greek word for "repent" is *metanoia*, from the words *meta*, "to change," and *noia*, "the breath." I love the idea of "repenting" to mean "changing the way you breathe."

Let's change the way we breathe. The next chapter will cover several different breathing techniques you can try, and you might just find they will change your life.

Conclusion

As you work to become better at deciphering divine guidance and your own intuition, remember to keep your focus on your breath. Oxygenating your body deeply every single day will help heighten your sensitivity over time and make it easier and easier to receive intuitive messages and recognize them for what they are. Head over to the next chapter for practical guidance on breathwork you can do right now to help deepen your ability to receive inspiration.

Chapter 3

Experiencing Pranayam

*P*ranayam is the yogic term for breathwork. And now that you understand how important it is to have your breath in order, it's time to learn some breathwork exercises, or pranayam, that you can start doing every day (or as often as you desire).

One of the best things you can do for your health—your spiritual, your emotional, your physical, *and* your mental health—is commit to spending at least five tiny minutes a day just focused on your breath.

These are a few breathing exercises that you can try. Each of them can be powerful. You can try them all in a row if you want, just a few breaths with each exercise, just to see how they feel. But it's also great to just try one exercise for the full five minutes, and try it just once or maybe try it a few days in a row and see how it makes you feel. But doing these exercises regularly can make a huge difference to your overall health *and* to your ability to hear divine guidance and intuitive answers.

With all of these exercises, be sure your posture is good: keep your back straight but relaxed, and your chest (or "heart center") open.

Long, Slow, Deep Breathing

This one is pretty self-explanatory, but I'll explain it anyway. With long, slow deep breathing, you want to breathe as slowly and deeply as possible. How long can you take to inhale? And how deeply can you inhale—can you feel the breath in the very depths of your lungs? And then, how slowly can you exhale it all out?

Doing five minutes of long, slow deep breathing can be hugely restorative during or at the end of a long day. Try it and see for yourself. Set that five minute timer and focus as exclusively as possible on just breathing as slowly and deeply as possible. How does that feel?

Single Nostril Breathing

When was the last time you breathed through only one nostril, on purpose?

For this exercise, sit with your back straight, and use your hand to plug just one nostril. Push the nostril down to close it, and breathe through the other nostril. Breathe as slowly and as deeply as possible.

Do this for 2.5 minutes, and then switch nostrils.

Breathing like this actually affects different areas of your brain. Sometimes this kind of breathwork can trigger an emotional release or lightheadedness. If you feel lightheaded, it's okay to stop and just go back to normal breathing.

Alternate Nostril Breathing

With this type of breathing, sit with your back straight and your hand close to your nose. Use your thumb and then your forefinger to plug first one nostril as you inhale, and then the other nostril as you exhale. Leave your finger there as you inhale through the same nostril you exhaled through, and then plug that nostril and exhale and inhale again through the other.

Breath of Fire

This way of breathing is intense, so do not do it if you are pregnant, menstruating, or recovering from significant illness.

The easiest way to learn the Breath of Fire is to start by panting like a dog, and then close your mouth, forcing the air in and out through your nose by contracting your abdominal muscles.

When you are breathing like this, *you* aren't really "breathing." Instead, when you squeeze your diaphragm inward, it creates a vacuum, and when you relax your diaphragm, it actually sucks air down into your lungs for you. Isn't that crazy?

This exercise can easily leave you feeling lightheaded, so if that happens, just stop and breathe normally. But Breath of Fire is an incredible way to purge carbon dioxide from your body, replenish yourself with oxygen, and get air into the deepest parts of your lungs.

Conclusion

These are just a few quick breath exercises that can help you heal your breathing. I recommend setting a timer for five minutes a day just to pay attention to your breathing—whether you do these exact exercises or not. But it is hard to become "inspired" when you are not a good breather!

Chapter 4

The Beliefs That Frame Your Experience

All of us experience life through the framework of our mental processes, also known as our subconscious programming. This means that whatever beliefs you have in your heart of hearts are the beliefs that color your experience of your life.

If you have a core belief that people are generally good and that they are all doing the best they can, when someone cuts you off in traffic, you're likely to think to yourself, "Oh no! That person must be having a health emergency! I hope they're okay!" And if you have a core belief that people are generally out to ruin your life, for example, when the exact same event of getting cut off in traffic happens, you're more likely to think to yourself, "That jerk! What a terrible person that just cut me off!" You might find yourself swearing either mentally or verbally, and you might actively wish harm on the other driver.

Wishing an irresponsible driver well or wishing them the worst life has to offer can both be reasonable responses to getting cut off in traffic; the only difference is where your mindset is coming from.

Our beliefs are everything when it comes to how we experience the world. This is true in traffic, it's true at school, it's true in your family, and it's true in the context of receiving divine revelation and intuitive guidance. If you have subconscious programs that say things like, "I can't hear divine guidance," "God never talks to me," or "God has abandoned me," of *course* you will struggle to feel like you are being divinely led. Even when you *are* being divinely led, your own subconscious programs and ways of thinking will block you from hearing that divine voice.

So how do you know if your beliefs have anything to do with your ability to hear or not-hear the voice of the Divine?

Well, this is something you would have to ask about... and receive an intuitive answer on! And if you're reading this book, you may struggle in that area.

So for the purposes of this book, I'm going to ask you to assume that you do have subconscious programming and mental beliefs that are keeping you from fully feeling led by the divine in your life. We are going to work through several exercises together to help you overcome this programming, and I'm excited for you to see for yourself how your life changes as you try this.

For these exercises, we are going to use a thing called "tapping." You may have heard of EFT, or Emotional Freedom Technique. We are not using EFT exactly. Instead, you will just use your fingertips to tap on your forehead, or your collarbone, or your knees, or anywhere on your body that is comfortable, while saying the various scripts out loud.

The scripts in this book have been designed to undo any negative programming around the idea of receiving divine guidance, and to add in positive programming that will support you in receiving the answers that you need.

Please read each script aloud a minimum of three times each, and please also remember that you may need to go through this list of scripts several times over the coming days and weeks and months in order to fully reprogram your mind. If any scripts feel wrong to you or out of alignment for you, just skip them.

Please take out your tapping fingers and "tap in" the following, by tapping your fingers on your body and speaking the following aloud three times each:

- Even though I have struggled to recognize divine guidance in the past, I am open to recognizing divine guidance now.

- Even though I have felt like I couldn't hear the voice of the Divine, I am open to hearing the voice of the Divine now.

- It could be safe for me to receive divine guidance.

- It could be safe for me to receive divine guidance in a way I natively understand.

- Even though I have felt like God must hate me, I deeply and completely love and accept myself.

- Even though I don't know how to release my feelings that God hates me, I find my body easily releasing those feelings and beliefs.

- Even though I have felt like a failure, I deeply and completely love and accept myself.

- Even though I don't know how to release my feelings of failure and accept that I am capable of hearing divine guidance, I deeply and completely love and accept myself.

- I don't know how I suddenly recognize intuitive insight when it comes to me now, I only know that I do recognize intuitive insight now.

- I don't know how intuitive insight and divine guidance flow so easily to me now, I only know they do flow easily to me now, and I am fulfilled.

- Even though my body has never known how to interpret the signals of divine energy, now my body is learning how to do it.

- My body is getting better and better every day at recognizing intuition and divine guidance.

- Every day I am getting better at listening to the still, small voice of divine guidance.

- Every day I am getting better at listening to my own intuition.

- It can be easy for me to discern between my thoughts and the voice of the Divine.

- I can easily tell when the divine is trying to communicate with me.

- Some other people easily experience divine guidance.

- I could possibly experience divine guidance.

- What would it feel like if I easily experienced divine guidance?

- What would it feel like if I easily experienced intuitive guidance?

- I choose to be open to easy, graceful divine guidance.

- I choose to be open to easy, graceful intuitive thoughts.

- It is safe for me to experience intuition and divine guidance because I can easily determine what is true guidance and what is not.

- Every day I learn more and more how to trust my own ability to hear divine guidance and intuitive guidance.

- I relax into my own intuition and wisdom in discerning divine guidance.

Assess Your Experience

As you go through these tapping scripts, how do you feel? Are there any scripts that are harder to tap in than others?

Pay attention to how easy or how hard it is to say the different words aloud. When you feel a natural struggle to get out certain sentences, that can be a signal that you have more going on there under the surface.

If that happens—if you start to struggle to say certain scripts—I urge you to write those scripts down, and then start asking questions. Why is this script hard to say? What in me might resist this concept, and why? Where do I feel the resistance to this in my body?

You can close your eyes and take your deep breath, and see if you can feel a very subtle feeling in your body when you work through these different scripts. When a script is hard, where in your body do you feel it—or where do you *imagine* that you feel it? Sometimes these feelings are so subtle, it feels almost more like an imaginary feeling than a real one. The secret is that even an imaginary feeling can count. We're working with very subtle energies, energies that can't be felt normally. We feel them with our spirit, and even with the imagination.

So feel out for yourself where in your body you feel any resistance to these tapping scripts. Understanding why you feel resistance can be helpful. To figure out why you feel that resistance, just ask yourself the question and release yourself from needing to know. See for yourself how over the next week or two, your brain will just gracefully bring to your conscious mind the answer. You will see for yourself how over time, just by asking yourself questions, your brain gently calls to you the answer in a way you can understand. And once you understand why you have resisted these things, you can consciously choose to let them go and breathe in a new belief.

Creating Your Own Tapping Scripts

You are absolutely capable of creating your own tapping scripts to help yourself overcome any false beliefs that are holding you back. Please refer back to the list I created for you, and create new variations that fit your own personal circumstance. See for yourself how you are brilliant and capable of coming up with exactly the right things to say to help reprogram your own body and mind to be more open to divine guidance.

Conclusion

If you have subconscious programming that keeps you in a space of doubt and rejection of divine guidance, of course you will struggle to feel led in your life! Please continue to go through these tapping scripts as often as necessary to help reroute your brain so you can easily and gently receive accurate intuitive answers.

Chapter 5

Your Body Is The Vessel

We experience intuitive insight and divine guidance through the medium of our physical bodies. It is our nervous system that picks up on spiritual information and translates it into physical and emotional feelings that we can then interpret. Of course, to call them "physical feelings" and "emotional feelings" is redundant. All emotions are also physical: all of our emotions are chemicals. Every emotion we experience is a chemical reaction inside of our brain and our gut, and that is what we interpret as our feelings. Are you happy? Or sad? Thank some chemicals and your nervous system.

Our physical bodies use chemicals and the medium of our nervous system to create the perceptions we have of spiritual insight. When it comes to receiving divine guidance and intuitive insight, we have to rely on our physical bodies. When we struggle to receive spiritual guidance, the first place to look must be the condition of our physical bodies. Indeed, in this book, we looked at the condition of our breathing as the very first thing. But up next must be the nervous system.

How is your nervous system?

Maybe you've seen the 2005 Keira Knightley Pride and Prejudice. I love that movie. And in that movie, Mrs. Bennet is always going on about her nerves. "My nerves!" she cries, every time something interesting happens. Check out this snippet from the script:

> **Mrs. Bennet:** Have you no consideration for my poor nerves?
>
> **Mr. Bennet:** You mistake me, my dear. I have the utmost respect for your nerves. They've been my constant companion these twenty years.

I love that! Every time I see this interaction in the movie, I laugh and laugh. And every time, I also think about my own nerves—and your nerves, too. Stress fries nervous systems, and when it does, we all become messes. Maybe we aren't running around like Mrs. Bennet, having conniptions and nervous breakdowns, but very often instead we exist in a state of low-level dysfunction, feeling exhausted on both a mental and physical body level.

If your nervous system is "fried," it will be much harder to use it to understand spiritual guidance. Even if the spiritual information is flowing to your body from the divine, if your nervous system is not prepared to pick up on it and translate that information into useful chemical signals that your brain can interpret, you will have a hard time. So the first thing to do, in my opinion, is focus on nervous system health.

To me, nervous system health has three major components: toxicity, nutrition, and emotional health. We have to address all three in order to have a fully functioning nervous system.

The Nervous System and Emotional Health

There is no such thing as strictly emotional stress. ALL stress becomes physical body stress, and that is all there is to it.

The body interprets stress as STRESS, regardless of whether that stress comes from feeling judged and unloved, or if it comes from being chased by a dinosaur or facing an ice age. All emotional stress becomes physical body stress. To the body, stress is stress and it results in the adrenal glands working overtime and an increase in cortisol in the body— cortisol that shuts down the digestive system, slows the metabolism, and draws fat to cortisol receptors in the belly and thighs. But this cortisol does so much more than just drive weight gain in some people. It also can throw off your nervous system and even your brain function, among many other things.

When we are emotionally stressed, our bodies pay the price for that. And when they do, it can show up in any number of ways. We experience physical symptoms of all kinds, ranging from digestive distress to weight problems to mental health crises and more; but we also experience nervous system overload that over time makes it very hard to hear divine guidance.

You can think of it like this: imagine a person trying to use a radio. They have a very important message they are trying to hear. But as they are trying to focus on the radio, kids come by and start screaming at each other, a dog starts barking, a train passes through and honks its horn... and imagine that this just never stops. The person trying to use the radio isn't doing anything wrong. They're doing it right. But the outside noise is just too much and the person can't hear the message.

This is what it is like trying to decipher divine guidance when our emotions are chronically unresolved.

How easy is it to hear what's being said on the "radio" when we have the loud noises of our emotional traumas going off within our bodies?

I am thinking back to a time where I had The Worst Job Ever and my entire life was falling apart. I would spend all day rotating mentally between the things that made me sad and the things that made me mad and the things that made me upset. I wasn't trying to be a Debbie Downer; it was just the natural consequence of having tons, tons, tons of stress in my life and not knowing how to remove it from my body. I would get stuck on depressing tracks of thought and not know how to stop and get off the train.

Virtually all humans have this problem. We are all physically and emotionally backlogged with stress, and this stress is not just an emotional feeling; it's a chemical reaction. And it is clogging up our systems and impairing our ability to "hear the radio" very clearly.

This is why it is so incredibly important to address our unhealed emotional issues.

I have numerous books available on Amazon and classes and by-donation sessions at allieduzettclasses.com that walk you through the process of releasing old emotional residue from your body, so I'm not going to delve deeply into it here. Please go visit my website and get started with the Free Offerings there to get this ball rolling. The important thing for you to understand here is that ANYTHING you do to heal yourself emotionally will help you in your quest to hear divine guidance.

Over the years I've been in this field, I've crafted hundreds of pre-recorded by-donation sessions for people to use to heal their emotions so they can heal their physical bodies. And because of the sheer volume of what is available, sometimes people can go into overwhelm: where do I start??

But the secret is: START ANYWHERE. Literally anything you do to reduce the emotional stress in your life is going to make a positive difference in your overall physical health, your overall emotional health, and in your ability to hear your own intuition and the voice of the Divine. So just get started! Don't be overwhelmed. Doing anything is a good choice.

Toxicity and the Nervous System

We live in a toxic world. The air we breathe is laced with gas fumes, car and airplane exhaust. The water we drink flows to us in lead pipes and comes filled with minute contaminants. The food we eat is all too often slathered in pesticides and herbicides, and wrapped in toxic plastic. We wear clothing made of artificial fibers and even petroleum. We eat, drink, breathe, and wear toxic material all day long every day. Many of us have also injected toxic materials into our bodies in the form of various vaccines. This takes an enormous toll on our physical bodies. And when our bodies are overwhelmed with toxicity, it doesn't just stress us out physically. It stresses us out emotionally.

This is because emotions are chemical. When our physical bodies are full of the chemicals of stress because of toxic exposure, well: stress is stress. Much of the emotional stress we carry day to day may actually have its root in toxic exposure.

One of the most important things we can do for our nervous systems is reduce our internal toxicity and our day-to-day toxic exposure. Learning more about endocrine disruptors and removing them from your lifestyle can be helpful. Many lotions and soaps contain toxic materials. Switching them out for more natural alternatives can be helpful. Some people make it a priority to only wear organic clothing. I don't. I have, however, removed all the plastic plates and bowls from my home. Even my little children eat off white glass Corelle plates (which are allegedly low in lead) and drink out of stainless steel cups instead of plastic. Filtering your water can be a good choice, and I don't have a recommendation on the perfect water filter. I urge you to do your own research.

But removing toxicity from our lives can only go so far. If we're still driving cars, we're still breathing fumes at the gas station. We can get air filters for our homes but we'll still go outside and breathe toxicity from the air outside.

For myself, while I limit my family's toxic exposure in the home within reason, I focus most on detoxing our physical bodies. My favorite product for detox is TRS, a tasteless, odorless zeolite detox spray that you take by spraying into your mouth. TRS stands for "**T**oxin and Contaminant **R**emoval **S**ystem" and it is manmade clinoptilolite zeolite suspended in water. I've included a section about this product in the back of the book. It is incredible for detoxing the nervous system directly. The link to order it is 412625.mycoseva.com.

Detoxing with TRS has led to massive healing in my home. In just my own personal family, we've seen eczema disappear forever, food allergies gone for good, asthma eradicated, constipation cleared, and more just from detoxing. TRS doesn't heal anything, but when a health problem has heavy metal toxicity as an underlying condition, detoxing can make a big difference. Remove the heavy metals, and the body heals itself.

If you have nervous system problems due to heavy metal toxicity, or toxicity from fluoride, chlorine, gadolinium, radioactive particles, or other toxic exposures, detoxing with TRS can help. You can see the back of the book for more information.

Other detoxing agents are activated charcoal, bentonite clay, and diatomaceous earth. Water that is high in silica, such as Fiji Water, can also be helpful in detoxing.

Nutrition and the Nervous System

Detoxing the nervous system is important, because as long as our bodies are clogged with toxicity, our nerves won't function properly. But just as important is nutrition.

Your entire life is a series of chemical reactions, and all of your feelings are a series of chemical reactions, too. All chemical reactions require ingredients. When your body lacks the appropriate ingredients for the desired result, the appropriate chemical reaction cannot happen.

This is a primary reason for depression, anxiety, and many mental health issues. How can your body create the chemicals of happiness in your brain if your diet does not supply those ingredients?

Processed "food" is a staple of many diets but processed "food" does not supply the ingredients necessary to have a properly functioning brain, nervous system, or body. I have to put the word "food" in quotations here because most of the processed products you can find at the grocery store do *not* qualify as actual life-giving food. They are merely food-like substances that fill our bellies and provide empty calories, often with a hefty dose of toxic poison as well. No wonder so many people are sick when the standard American diet is filled with ingredients that don't support the chemical reactions of health.

On the other side of the equation, however, flooding our bodies with nutrients allows our bodies to heal and flourish. On a physical body level, just eating the proper amounts of necessary nutrients can allow the nerves and brain and other key organs to heal, because they finally have the ingredients necessary to do so.

Beyond that, on a religious level, the connection between food and the internal spirit is a staple of many religions. Many religions have strict dietary rules, such as Judaism and Islam. Many religions support fasting, or abstaining from food for a set period of time, as a way to connect more deeply with the Divine.

In the Holy Bible, Daniel in the Book of Daniel shows his devotion to God through his rigorous devotion to his diet, and to this day, many people claim that adhering to a diet similar to Daniel's can lead to a deeper spiritual connection.

This makes a lot of sense. Our bodies are machines and they need the right ingredients to function properly.

Leafy greens are full of vitamin B, which supports nerve function, and alpha-lipoic acid, which also prevents nerve damage and helps promote proper nerve function. Fruits and vegetables high in antioxidants, like berries and zucchini, help promote proper nerve health. Some berries, like cranberries and blueberries, naturally contain high amounts of a chemical called resveratrol, which is amazing for reducing inflammation. Healthy fats are critical to a functional nervous system, so avocado and wild caught fish can be a great addition to the diet. All foods high in vitamins A and C, like the sweet potato, serve the nervous system.

This is a list of some foods that support a healthy nervous system:

- Leafy greens and dark green vegetables of all kinds, including asparagus, kale, spinach, broccoli, and more
- Avocado
- Quinoa
- Sweet potato
- Zucchini
- Berries of all kinds
- Grapes
- Melons of all kinds
- Fatty fish, including salmon, tuna, mackerel, trout, and sardines
- Organic meats, like grass-fed beef and pastured chicken and pork
- Nuts

I always tell my kids that they have to eat foods that were alive once. This is a pretty good rule. Your Doritos were not alive once (there is not a Dorito farm), but your steak and potatoes once were alive. Eating foods that lived once is a great rule of thumb to be sure that your body is able to receive the nutrients it needs.

My degree is in soil sciences, and way back in the olden days when I was at university, my teachers even back then would talk about the distressing state of the soil and therefore the distressing state of the nutrients in our food.

The food we eat has to get its nutrients from the soil, but in the past several decades, our soil has gotten extremely depleted. In my opinion, this has a lot to do with modern farming techniques but also the modern lifestyle of throwing away food instead of returning it to the Earth. When we toss our leftovers in the trash, instead of the compost pile, the nutrients from that food ends up sequestered in a garbage bag in a landfill, instead of returning to the farming ecosystem. This has never been done before; historically, nutrients were always returned to the system in one way or another. But now we are losing access to the nutrients in food waste at an alarming rate.

Modern fertilizers provide the three main nutrients necessary for plant life: potassium, nitrogen, and phosphorus. But many *micro*nutrients are necessary for not just life, but health, and those micronutrients are typically not added into any fertilizers. We are growing plants that are big and beautiful-looking, but very low in the necessary nutrients to keep our bodies thriving and functional.

In a study called *Changes in USDA Food Composition Data for 43 Garden Crops, 1950 to 1999* by Donald R. Davis, Melvin D. Epp, and Hugh D. Riordan, they found that in just 50 years, vitamin C levels in garden crops dropped 15%, vitamin B2 levels dropped 38%, protein content dropped 6%, iron content dropped 15%, calcium content dropped 16%, and phosphorus content dropped 9%.

That seems bad, but other studies have pegged the numbers at even worse rates. An analysis from the Kushi Institute found that from 1975 to 1997, calcium levels in vegetables dropped 27%, iron levels dropped a whopping 37%, vitamin A levels dropped 21%, and vitamin C levels dropped 30%.

Another study found that on the average, food now is about 38% less nutritious than it was 50+ years ago.

Whoever is doing the analyzing, it appears that the science is clear: our food is becoming less nutritious. They say that you would have to eat eight of today's oranges to get the same amount of vitamin A as our grandparents would have received from one single orange.

In order to get the same amount of nutrients as our grandparents did, we would have to eat many times more fruits and vegetables than they needed to. It is not realistic to do this for most people! Want to eat 8 oranges today to hit your vitamin A goals?

Supplementation to me is NOT optional. This is actually why I started my work as a medical intuitive in the first place. In the beginning of my work, I did all my sessions for free, but as my reputation increased and the demand for my time grew, I realized that I was going to have to get a job if I was going to keep up with my body's accompanying demand for nutrients. It is almost impossible to be a functional medical intuitive without a functional nervous system, and a functional nervous system needs plenty of vitamins! It was the drive to be able to afford vitamins that prompted me to initially begin charging for my work: I realized that if I was going to be able to provide high quality intuitive information to people, I had to take care of my physical body. And so I needed to be able to afford the supplements I would need to keep my nerves in tip-top shape.

For me, some critical nutrients to supplement include:

- **Vitamin C.** This water-soluble vitamin is necessary for functional cell walls and for a strong immune system. Your entire body benefits from receiving sufficient vitamin C. When you are sick you need more vitamin C than when you are healthy. You cannot overdose on vitamin C; when you take too much, you'll just pee and poop out the excess. This is the way to make sure you're getting enough vitamin C: by taking it to "bowel tolerance." Especially when you aren't feeling well, taking enough vitamin C to make your bowels a little rumbly and gassy, but not diarrheal, can ensure that you're getting enough vitamin C to promote healing. I don't have a preferred brand of vitamin C. I personally use NOW brand ascorbic acid powder, which I mix into water and drink as tart lemonade, even though I know that whole food vitamin C is better (such as powdered acerola cherry).

For my kids, I buy chewables without lots of fillers and I avoid all artificial coloring in their chewables.

- **Magnesium.** It takes 43 molecules of magnesium to process 1 molecule of sugar. If you've ever eaten an Oreo, but didn't supplement with magnesium afterwards, you are magnesium deficient. Magnesium is absolutely critical to nerve function and overall health. Magnesium helps support something like 500+ known functions in the body. So catching up on your magnesium supplementation can be a game changer. Like vitamin C, excess magnesium will just end up excreted by the bowels—that was a nice way to say, if you take too much magnesium, you'll get diarrhea. But this is also another way of pointing out, if you deal with chronic constipation problems, you may *actually* be dealing with chronic vitamin C and magnesium deficiency. My preferred brand of magnesium is called Jigsaw. I usually take between 4-10 Jigsaw SRT magnesium tablets before bed every night. You can order these off many websites that sell supplements.

- **MSM.** MSM stands for methylsulfonylmethane, which is exactly why people call it MSM. It is essentially a methylated sulfur. MSM reduces joint pain and inflammation, increases glutathione levels, helps heal muscle damage, reduces allergic symptoms, boosts the immune system, and improves skin health. I seriously feel amazing when I am on top of my MSM supplementation. I prefer MSM in capsules, instead of tablets.

- **Turmeric**. Turmeric is a spice often used in curry. It turns everything it touches yellow. And it is a massively powerful anti-inflammatory. It contains curcumin, a nutrient that can be so helpful in healing many aspects of your body. Taking a high quality turmeric supplement can be life-changing. I love the turmeric supplement from Vidafy. I love it so much I became a distributor. The link to order is: https://www.vidafy.info//link/page/ALLIEDUZETT. Go to that link, click "buy now," "Bioms," and Curcuma Plus is the product I am crazy about. My husband had frozen shoulder for years—a condition caused by chronic inflammation of the bursa in the shoulder. The condition will persist until the inflammation clears. And it wasn't clearing no matter what we did! But just a week on Curcuma Plus and his shoulder went back to normal. I am a huge believer in the power of Vidafy's Curcuma Plus to help reduce inflammation in a massive way.

- **Amino acids**. Having the proper amount of amino acids is critical for brain health. Amino acids are the precursors to the brain chemicals you need to have a functional memory, multitask, plan ahead, sleep well, and just generally be happy and feel a sense of wellbeing. I'm not an amino acids expert by any means, but I do love them and believe in them. Some years ago, I met Shelly Jo Wahlstrom, the creator of HypnoAminos (a brand of amino acids). She was a hypnotherapist who discovered that hypnotherapy was incredibly more powerful for healing when combined with amino acid supplementation. She was able to help many people heal from "incurable" mental health conditions using this combination of emotional healing work and amino acids. One of the best things about amino acid supplementation is that it does not have to last forever. If you can supplement consistently for a few years (like maybe 3 years), it supports your brain to be able to maintain its own amino acid balance. So this particular kind of supplementation doesn't have to be forever. I have loved the amino acids from hypnoaminos.com.

- **Fulvic acid**. Fulvic acid is absolutely miraculous when it comes to healing the body, because it is made up of the micronutrients mostly missing from our food today. Even a drop or a tiny pinch of fulvic acid can make a huge difference for your body. Some people see and experience big body changes after their first ingestion of fulvic acid. Fulvic acid essentially supercharges the cells and the mitochrondria to support full body cellular health. When I take it, I feel energized and calm. My preferred brand of fulvic acid is Advanced Fulvic from Coseva. The link to order is awinegarduzett.mycoseva.com. I've tried several different brands of fulvic acid but keep going back to that one! Coseva has used nanotechnology to nano-ize the fulvic acid so it is extra bioavailable, and I can really tell the difference. One dropperful can go a long way!

- **Collagen.** Collagen contains the nutrients needed for nerve *regeneration*, which is great news if you have nerve damage. Collagen is also a main ingredient in fascia, the thing that when lumped up from trauma creates cellulite. Those bumps are not fat; it's lumped-up fascia. When your body has access to lots of collagen, it can start proactively releasing the old damaged fascia and nerve cells, and replacing them with new ones. Some people report big emotional shifts when they start taking collagen, for this reason. Old emotions can be stored in bunched up fascia, and when your body naturally heals that fascia, it clears out the chemicals of those old emotions as well. There are lots of collagen supplements out there all claiming to be the super best. I am not a collagen connoisseur. I know it gets a bad rap out there in the MLM collagen world, but I often use Vital Proteins brand of unflavored collagen, which I obtain from Costco. It's not the highest quality collagen in the world but I feel good on it. I mix it with raw cacao and DandyBlend roasted dandelion root powder to make a delicious, high-protein breakfast drink that also detoxes my liver. I also like the Kyani brand of collagen, HL5. When I remember, I take 2 pouches a day. I don't remember all the time so it probably evens out to be about 1 pouch a day.

- **Cardio Miracle**. I just started taking Cardio Miracle and immediately after taking it I felt so much better in my body. The first day I had Cardio Miracle, I took 6 scoops of it and felt amazing. This is a delicious drink powder that is high in vitamins and minerals and nitric oxide. Everything in it is supportive to a healthy nervous system.

Conclusion

Your nervous system health is essential to perceiving spiritual direction. In order to have a healthy and functional nervous system, addressing diet, toxic exposure, and emotional health is *absolutely critical and non-negotiable.*

Chapter 6

Strengthening the Nervous System

We've talked about how important it is to breathe, detox, eat nutritional food, supplement, and address your emotional trauma. All of these things are key to strengthening and healing your physical body and priming you to be in a space where your nervous system can easily pick up on the spiritual information surrounding you every day.

The final piece of the puzzle is actually strengthening and toning the nervous system. You can be fully detoxed, have lots of great nutrition, be totally clear of emotional trauma, and be breathing very deeply, but if your nerves are not toned, you may still have problems accessing intuitive information.

You can think of this like playing a difficult sport. All the sports are difficult for me (ha!) but I'll compare it to rock climbing.

You can be eating exclusively high-nutrient foods, and you can have zero toxic exposure, no emotional health issues to speak of, and great breath control, but you will *still* have troubles climbing up the sheer face of a cliff if you don't have the proper musculature to support the adventure.

Your nerves are the muscles of your intuitive ability. You *must* strengthen and tone your nerves if you are going to be effective at feeling, recognizing, and interpreting spiritual information.

So how do you strengthen your physical nerves?

Yoga for the Nervous System

I hope it is no surprise to you that yoga is an exceptional form of exercise for the nervous system. Yoga was actually designed with the specific purpose of healing the nerves. All kinds of yoga are fabulous for the nervous system, and if you can only do one thing to actively strengthen your nervous system, I would say to do five or ten minutes a day of yoga—or, if "yoga" isn't your thing, let's just call it "stretching." Stretching your body for a few minutes a day can lead to big gains in strength where your nerves are concerned.

Here are some of the best yoga moves—or stretches—you can do to help heal your nervous system. I'm not really a yoga *or* stretching teacher so please have grace with these explanations! They are basic and may not be perfect but they will still get the job done if you do them.

> **Seated Spinal Twist** The seated spinal twist stimulates your immune system as well as your

nervous system. Start seated criss-cross applesauce, or in a chair if criss-cross applesauce is too much for you. Sit with your spine straight. Gently twist your upper body to the left, and place your right hand on the outside of your left knee to help lengthen the stretch. Hold for a few deep breaths. Then twist back to center. Breathe, and then do the stretch to the right.

Cat-Cow This exercise is one of my favorites. Start on your hands and knees. Lift your head, lengthening your neck, and then on the exhale tilt your head down and round your back, tucking your tailbone under. On the inhale stretch out your chest, stretch your spine, and look straight ahead again. Do this for a few minutes and see how energized you feel.

Side Moons This exercise is similar to Cat-Cow, but instead of moving your head and spine up and down, you move from side to side. Start on hands and knees, but curl your hips and shoulders towards each other on the right side, and then curl your hips and shoulders towards each other on the left side. Synchronize your inhales and exhales with the movement.

Downward Dog To do this stretch, start on all fours. Then raise your hips to the sky while straightening your legs. Come back down on all fours to get out of the stretch.

Happy Baby Pose Lie down on your back and put your feet in the air. Bend your knees to bring your feet closer to your. Reach out and grab your big toes using your index fingers. Breathe. You can rock back and forth a little in this position as well.

Legs Up On a Wall This stretch is what it sounds like! Lie down and put your sit bones against a wall, and your legs up against the wall. Breathe. This pose is very soothing for the nerves, and also especially for the female reproductive system.

Arm Swinging In kundalini yoga (my favorite type of yoga), yoga postures are dynamic, and you move around quite a bit. To do this exercises, straighten your arms so they are parallel with the ground and place your left hand over your right hand and interlace your fingers. Then, twist your entire torso left and right, your neck and head aligned with the movement. Keep your elbows straight and do the back and forth movement quickly. This strengths your chest muscles and pumps the lymph in that area.

Child's Pose This pose helps calm the digestive system, as well as stimulate the nervous system. Start in a kneeling position, and then bend forward until your forehead touches the ground. Breathe deeply.

Corpse Pose This is the most important pose of all. After you stretch your body, it's important to give your body a rest period to reintegrate. To do corpse pose, just lie on the floor with your arms and legs outstretched, and breathe deeply, focusing on your breath. Doing this for a few minutes at the end of any exercise can help your nerves and energy field heal up and integrate all the body-level information you unlocked through your stretches and other exercise.

These are just a few stretches you can do to support your nerves. Realistically, any yoga or stretching that you do will be helpful to you! One great place to look for additional stretches is 3ho.com. Go there and search for yoga and meditations to support the nervous system and try the ones that come up.

Humming and Singing

Humming doesn't sound like an exercise, but it actually is and it specifically strengthens the vagus nerve, which is one of the most important nerves in your body. Can you hum for five minutes today, with the intention that your humming is strengthening and toning your vagus nerve?

Singing also can help tone the vagus nerve. This nerve connects in on the other side of your throat, by the spine and your brain. So activating the back your throat by singing and humming strengthens that whole area and helps the vagus nerve be that much more effective. The vagus nerve is the one that connects your brain to all the rest of the stuff you've got going on in your body, so it's pretty critical. And studies have shown that having a weak vagus nerve is linked to anxiety, depression, and basically all the sad, bad feelings you don't like to feel.

So sing and hum with intention: this can help your vagus nerve!

Gargling

Gargling water in the back of your throat also doesn't sound like an exercise, but it actually is. And what it strengthens is, again, the vagus nerve. This is one exercise that many doctors recommend specifically for toning that critical vagus nerve that helps moderate all other nerve activity in the body.

You can gargle regular water or salt water, or whatever else you feel like you would like to gargle, although for me I can't imagine what else might be worth gargling. But try gargling for just thirty seconds in a row (or just ten, if thirty is too much!) and try building up over time to two minutes. You can build a lot of vagal tone in just a few minutes a day with some high quality daily gargling.

Other Nerve Strengthening Exercises

As it turns out, virtually all exercise helps strengthen your nerves. But specific types of exercise that many sources recommend for nerve strengthening include running, walking, jogging, bicycling, and swimming. Lifting weights is an excellent way to strengthen your nervous system. And one specific exercise that many doctors recommend for nervous system tone is pull-ups: pull-ups help activate and strengthen many aspects of your overall nervous system.

Physical body exercise is about more than just being skinny or looking hot. Physical body exercise is important also because it strengthens your nerves and your nerves are what enable you to decipher divine direction.

What exercises do you enjoy? What exercise can you start building into your life for just five minutes a day?

Shaking It Out

Literally just shaking your body can strengthen and tone your nerves! I do this a lot. Just wiggling, or putting on some music and dancing, can be really helpful to your nerve health. This is a great way to clear old emotions out of your system as well.

In nature, when animals experience a high stress moment, such as almost getting hit by a car, afterwards, they will shake and shake. These shakes are called "neurogenic tremors." Perhaps you have experienced them—I've been in a handful of minor car accidents in my life and each time afterwards my body would just tremble for an hour or so. Trembling is an excellent way to literally "shake out" trauma from the nervous system and strengthen the nerves.

Trembling can be a natural response to certain forms of stress, but when you're not naturally trembling, you can mimic it by just shaking your body on purpose, consciously. Try setting a timer for 1 minute, and setting the intention to shake something out of your nervous system in that time. Then just purposely tremble your own hands and arms, to start with (it's easier to just do this with your arms and hands than with your entire body, especially if you're new to this form of exercise). See what happens when you tremble on purpose and what differences you notice in your feelings.

Cold Showers

I really admire the work of Wim Hof, the Ice Man, and I recommend his book, The Wim Hof Method. He teaches people how to withstand extreme cold by training the body with just a few minutes of cold showering every day.

Cold showers can be massively healing, because they train the vascular system of the body. All of our body is filled with tiny capillaries that carry blood everywhere—and because in the modern world, we are warm virtually all the time, that capillary system is typically weak and flaccid for most people.

Taking cold showers exercises this system and makes it strong. When it is strong, you can more easily withstand stress of *all* kinds. Yes, it makes it so you can easily withstand cold temperatures outside, but it also makes it so you can more easily withstand the emotional stress of your life.

Taking cold showers also helps tone the nervous system. Cold showers have long been recommended by yogic masters for that reason.

Take your normal shower, but at the end of it, shift the water to cold. When the water shifts, you will involuntarily suck in a huge, loud gasp of air. Sink into your breath while you allow the cold water to glide down your back. Start by doing this for 10-30 seconds, and build up to 2 minutes over a few weeks.

One person I know started doing this as a way to handle postpartum psychosis, and it really helped. It's a way to quickly shift emotional states and move old trauma out of your nervous system, while also strengthening your nervous system.

For a full explanation and many reasons why cold showering is amazing, check out The Wim Hof Method book.

Additional Nerve Strengthening Activities

You'll be pleased to hear that some "exercises" that help strengthen the nervous system hardly feel like exercise at all. Merely going outside barefoot on grass or rock or soil can help tone the nervous system, because electrons from the earth's surface will transfer into the soles of your feet, and support nervous system health on an atomic level.

Standing in the sun for 15 minutes a day promotes the creation of vitamin D, which helps support nervous system health as well.

Meditation can be strengthening to the nerves. I prefer kundalini meditation and have tutorials for several meditations, including the Kirtan Kriya, on my Youtube Channel (Allie Duzett: Medical Intuitive).

Conclusion

Strengthening your nervous system is absolutely imperative if you struggle to discern spiritual answers. Even if your body is in terrible condition, there are still things you can do for yourself—like getting into the sunlight for a few minutes a day, or stretching whatever muscles you are capable of. I'm thinking of my grandfather, who was paralyzed for a few years a child with rheumatic fever. During those years, he only had access to one set of muscles: his neck. So since he couldn't move anything else, he would stretch and exercise his neck muscles. When he finally regained control of his limbs, he had one very powerful and muscular neck!

If you can't do much with your physical body, I urge you to think of whatever it is that you *can* do, and start with that. Do not allow feelings of hopelessness to keep you from the small and simple things you could get started with right now.

You will see for yourself that increasing your nerve tone assists you in all areas of your life.

Chapter 7

Harnessing the Conductor

Why did we just spend so much time talking about nervous system health in a book about hearing spiritual guidance?

The answer lies with **electricity**.

We are electrical beings. We run on electricity. On a cellular level, our cells themselves run on electricity. Cellular respiration, also known as oxidative phosphorylation, is the term for how our cells create ATP, the energy we use to survive. During this process, the mitochondria inside your cells work as little batteries, and use literal electrical voltages to create ATP.

We are electric.

For me, I personally believe this is because spirits are electrical. And because our spirits are electrical and spiritual information is electrical, we need the part of us in charge of deciphering electrical signals to be strong and robust. And that part of us is our nervous system.

The Electrical Nature of Spirits

When my "third eye" first opened when I was 25, I was stunned to discover that we are absolutely surrounded by spiritual beings at all times.

I found that each human has two separate guardian angels, whose only job is to protect the physical body during this mortal endeavor. Beyond guardian angels, we have spirit guide angels that are helping with more spiritual endeavors— what I mean by this is, your guardian angels would help you avoid a car accident, but your spirit guides would help you get into the right college or meet your future spouse at the right time.

I saw that each mother has angels assigned over her motherhood, with each child being assigned some angels that are specific to that child's childhood and their connection with their mother. I call these "mother's helper angels."

There are many more angels that surround us every day, at least in my observation, but there are *also* negative entities, or what you might call evil spirits, and even ghosts (which to me are two separate classifications).

When I first started being able to see spirits, I saw many angels, and I saw many of the opposite!

My understanding is that angels are human spirits that are connected with this earth: either they already lived on this earth and died, and now their spirit acts in an angelic capacity for their descendants, *or* angels can also be people that haven't been born yet. So you could have an as-yet-unborn child acting as an angel for you for some time—and conversely, *you* could have been an angel for someone else before you were born. I write about this at length in my book Deep Past Resolution, because I feel strongly that many of our issues here on earth have stemmed from experiences as angels for others before we were born. I don't personally believe in reincarnation, but I do believe that people have legitimate "past life" memories. I believe these memories stem from having been angels to other people in the past.

I mention this because evil spirits have never lived on this earth. My understanding is that these are the spirits who chose to follow the devil in the war discussed in Revelation 12 in the Holy Bible. These spirits have never lived a mortal life, and never will. Their job on this earth is to interfere with people and try to basically ruin their lives, get them to suffer and make choices they regret. And just as each person is surrounded with angels, many of us are also surrounded with evil spirits.

Ghosts, to me, are the disembodied spirits of the deceased who have not crossed back "across the veil" to become angels. Their spirits remain trapped on this earth. So those are the three classifications of unseen spirits, to me.

But I mention all of this because when I was new at seeing spirits, and I started seeing evil spirits a lot, I would cast them out, Bible-style. I would tell them to "get thee hence" and cast them out when I found them—only to discover that my electronics would have a hard time. I would cast out an evil spirit from someone in my home, but then my garage door would stop working, in that very minute. I started having car troubles and troubles with all sorts of electronics.

I called my aunt, who has similar skills, and she explained that if you don't cast out evil spirits and specifically ban them from returning to people *or electronics*, they will end up lodged in your electronics.

And sure enough, shortly after this conversation, I went to the bank. I was in the drive-through of it, and I told the lady my name, and she couldn't find my account. I had handed over my drivers license but still she couldn't find my account. This started taking a really long time.

I prayed and asked God what was going on—and when I did, I suddenly saw the face of an evil spirit laughing at me from inside the computer the bank teller was working on. I cast out the evil spirit from the computer, and literally in that moment, she found my account. It had been there all along.

There's a lot to be learned from this story, but the important thing for this conversation is: an evil spirit was *in a computer*, because computers are electrical.

The important thing is: spirits are electrical. We feed off of electricity.

This electrical nature also explains why ghosts are typically seen on "dark and stormy nights" instead of bright and sunny days. During storms, electrical energy is heightened, and water is a conductor of electricity. Disembodied spirits on the earth can draw on that electrical storm energy and use the conductive power of ambient water to temporarily become visible.

I grew up in Maryland, and several times had the chance to go on the ghost tour in Harpers Ferry, West Virginia. I still go on that ghost tour as often as possible! I love it! But as a child I would always wonder why that area had so, so many ghost sightings.

Now I believe it is because of several reasons. First, the extreme trauma of the Civil War in that area had many people die and go right into shock. My understanding is that every spirit needs to go through "the tunnel of light" after they die, to get to the "other side of the veil," or you could call it the angelic dimension. But the tunnel of light only persists for a few days after a person's death. And death doesn't just automatically change people. If you have a traumatic death, you may be spiritually and emotionally in trauma as a result of that, and in that case, you might be too traumatized to actually go to the tunnel of light and pass through it. Then, once it closes, you're trapped here on this earth, and you've still got all your trauma. Trauma is electrical in nature, too. So we have these highly-charged, traumatized ghosts from the Civil War in Harpers Ferry.

But on top of that, Harpers Ferry is surrounded by rivers. I believe the highly saturated air of the area provides the hydroelectricity needed for ghosts to appear. Why? Because water is a conductor of electricity.

And *that* is the really important thing you need to know.

Water as the Conductor

Our spirits run on electricity, and spiritual information is transmitted electrically. We are surrounded by electrical impulses—ambient spiritual information—and our ability to perceive them is linked to the health of our nervous systems. This is because our nervous systems are in charge of perceiving electrical signals.

Having a strong and functional nervous system is a significant part of the equation, but another part of this equation is **hydration**.

Water is a conductor of electricity. When we are chronically dehydrated, we're not just killing ourselves slowly by depriving our vital organs of the water they need to survive. We are *also* impairing our ability to perceive spiritual information.

When we go for long periods of time without sufficiently hydrating, our bodies truly suffer from it. To survive, our organs do what it takes to get by on less water—but they are not happy. They trade in functionality for survival, and your body, *and* your ability to perceive spiritual information, suffers because of it.

By the time you feel thirsty, your body has already been suffering the effects of dehydration for some time. Digestion is such an important process, your body will shuffle around water from your internal organs to try to function long before it will take water from your mouth and throat. When you are thirsty, it is absolutely time to drink as much as you can.

We currently live in a world with abundant access to beverages of all kinds... but most of those beverages will actually *dehydrate* you when you drink them.

Soda pop, coffee, and even fruit juices can be *dehydrating* and when we drink them, even though we are drinking, it's not serving or healing our bodies. So we are in a curious situation where many people are drinking beverages all day long, but still suffering the effects of chronic dehydration.

Hydrating beverages include water, herbal infusions (herbal teas), bone and meat broth, and raw milk.

Rules for Getting Hydrated

The rule of thumb is that every person needs to consume half their body weight in ounces of water every day. In other words, if you weigh 100 pounds, you need to drink 50 ounces of water a day, at minimum. If you weigh 200 pounds, you need to drink a minimum of 100 ounces of water a day.

But if you drink any dehydrating beverages, such as a Coke or a cup of coffee, you then need to add in 1.5 times as much water as the amount of the beverage you drank.

So as an example, say you weigh 150 pounds, and therefore you need to drink 75 ounces of water every day. But you kick off the day with 8 ounces of coffee. To make up for the coffee you drank, now on top of the 75 ounces of water, you need, you need to drink an additional 12 ounces of water (which is 1.5x the amount of coffee you drank), for a total of 87 ounces of water on top of the 8 ounces of coffee.

Say that later in the day you have a 12-ounce bottle of Sprite. Then to make up for that, you will need to drink an additional 18 ounces of water. Your 8 ounces of coffee and your 12 ounces of Sprite added a total of 30 ounces of water to your needed amount for the day. If you had just had water, you would have needed just 75 ounces of water to be hydrated throughout the day, but because of the additional beverages, now you need 105 ounces of water—and you've already had 20 ounces of beverages. That's a lot of drinking!

When your body has been chronically dehydrated, it can take a while for your body to trust that you are going to seriously rehydrate it and stay on top of your hydration. It takes a minimum of three weeks of daily hydration, not missing a day, to rebuild that trust with your body. Once you do that, though, you may find that you release some excess water weight from water your body had to keep in storage because you weren't drinking enough. You will find that your mind is clearer and your emotions are more stable.

The body has limited ways to connect with us, and it's not like it can just tell us to consciously think, "Drink more water!" Instead, the body communicates with physical body feelings like thirst, inflammation, and physical pain when it is chronically dehydrated—and it also communicates dehydration with feelings of anxiety. The physical body will release the chemicals of anxiety when it is anxious for water. When we don't know this, we can assume we have an anxiety disorder or anxiety problems instead of just chronic dehydration. So you may find that once you attend to your body's needs for water with consistency and diligence, that many of your emotions start evening out and becoming more manageable as well.

Electrolyte Needs

Just drinking water without electrolytes can cause problems for some people. Like me! I have been "some people" in this example!

I tend to drink massive, massive amounts of water. But during my fourth pregnancy, it started causing me real problems. Drinking tons of water without increasing my mineral intake led to the water essentially washing out my minerals, and counterintuitively, my obsession with hydration led to more health problems. These problems were easily solved with the addition of mineral supplementation. At the time I took Organa brand peach-mango flavored minerals, which I found at my local grocery store. Now I take Advanced Fulvic drops from Coseva (awinegarduzett.mycoseva.com).

Early on, when my electrolyte imbalance was more severe, I would use electrolyte mixes I bought at Costco in my water. I don't like those because they are very sweet for me, but they are better than nothing if you need electrolyte support.

Gatorade markets itself as an electrolyte drink, but all of my own study has led me to believe Gatorade is one of the *least* helpful things you can drink for your hydration.

When I don't have access to other minerals or electrolyte supplements, often I will just salt my water—literally, I will sprinkle my water with salt and drink it. I use high quality salts

(Himalayan and Redmond salt), not cheap gross stuff. Having enough salt helps your body moderate its water.

Electrolytes are important because you need minerals to keep your tissues healthy. Plain water can end up washing out your minerals, but electrolyte supplementation can help.

Another reason to stay on top of electrolyte intake is that electrolytes in water actually make the water more electrically conductive. And that is helpful for spiritual connectivity.

Hydration for Spiritual Connection

Because water is a conductor of electricity, when we are fully hydrated, it means all of our physical body tissues are permeated with a conductor. Especially when we have a good mineral and electrolyte balance as well as proper hydration, it means our entire bodies become a conductive vessel. When our Higher Power or our Higher Self sends us spiritual information—which, remember, is *electrical*—our nerves can more easily pick up on it.

I'm usually pretty compassionate and sympathetic to people's problems, but there is a part of me I call "Tough Love Allie," and Tough Love Allie tells it like it is.

Tough Love Allie has ZERO time for people struggling to hear divine guidance who are not putting in the effort to maintain proper hydration.

If you are not drinking sufficient amounts of water every day, of course you will struggle to perceive spiritual information. Step one: drink more water.

A Note About Types of Water

Of course, not all water is created equal! This is just a quick note on water quality.

The first thing I have to do is of course caution you against reverse osmosis systems. To me, these are incredibly dangerous. Drinking only reverse osmosis water for an extended period of time (several months), without careful attention to mineral intake, is a recipe for serious health disasters. Don't take my word for it. You can go online and just use your favorite search engine to look up the health risks of reverse osmosis water. I would never use reverse osmosis myself.

Some years ago I read an excellent book called The Blue Death. This book is about the history of waterborne illness, and the disturbing conclusion of the book takes a look at the modern history of water filtration in America. The short version is: the water from your tap is NOT well cleaned, at least not as well cleaned as you would assume it or hope it to be. It is absolutely worth it to use filtered water.

Fridge filters aren't the super best, but they will filter out chlorine and some other things, which is good. When taking fulvic acid supplements, it's important to take them with unchlorinated water, a fridge-filtered water is sufficient for that.

For years I used a Berkey water filter, until we moved and it wouldn't fit on my counter. Now information has come out about Berkey filters possibly not filtering out fluoride as claimed, and you can investigate that for yourself. I'm not an expert in it.

These days, because of my housing situation (meaning: my countertop being extremely small with no place for a good filter), I do just use tap and fridge water, and I just take a lot of daily TRS to detox any metals or other positively-charged material I might be ingesting from my water.

I recently bought a Community LifeStraw filter to use in the case of an emergency.

I also have a Somavedic EMF-neutralizer that claims also to restructure water. I will be honest and admit that I haven't used it very much for that! Although I have noticed it helping with my EMF sensitivity and I've been thinking about getting another Somavedic for my bedroom.

Some people swear by Kangen water and other alkalizing water systems. I'm not an expert in that.

Really, I invite you to do your own research on the kind of water you want in your life. Just know that not all water is created equal and it's important to find a solution for water intake that works *for you* and your unique needs.

Conclusion

Water is the bridge between our physical bodies and our spiritual connectivity. It makes a lot of sense that people who struggle to maintain proper hydration and electrolyte intake often also struggle to feel connected spiritually. Addressing this physical body issue can make some serious spiritual impact as well.

Chapter 8

Accessing the Divine Polarity

I've never written my own story down before, but I guess this is a perfect place to do it. I often say that my "third eye just woke up one day," but that's not entirely true. It's not entirely true because of all the other stuff I wrote about in this book so far.

As you know, my name is Allie Duzett, and *now* I work as a medical intuitive and astrologer. But obviously that was not my job forever! Ten years ago, I was still in a space where I wasn't sure all of this stuff was even real. I earned a Bachelors of Science in environmental science, emphasis soil sciences, from Brigham Young University in 2009, and I was raised (and still am) very religious. My science background left me skeptical of claims of auras and chakras, and my Christian faith had left me believing that even if those things *were* real, maybe it was wrong to work with them.

But one day, my perspective shifted—because suddenly I literally *could see* the unseen world: auras, chakras, spirits, angels, and the spiritual component of people's physical health issues. I could see it all. I was stunned.

At the time, I didn't know why this had happened. What I *did* know is that I have a genius IQ, I'm very emotionally stable, and I am a deeply good person. Not to toot my own horn or something, but I just knew that I have always prioritized prayer and scripture study, I have always prioritized my religious observance, and—let's put it this way—I know my own heart, and my own intentions, and my intentions are and always have been *good*. At least in my own opinion.

So when I saw a person's aura for the first time, I was shocked and stunned, but I did know that I was not crazy, that I was very smart, and that I was a good person. I assumed that therefore what I was experiencing was legitimate, and that God wouldn't have let me experience it unless it was for some greater good of some kind. So I just decided to experiment with it, study it out, and connect with God every day to figure out what had happened and how to use it.

Fast forward a few years, and here we are. But that is how it all started.

Except, that's not the full story. Because my third eye opened like that only *after* a few things... things I didn't understand the significance of at the time.

The Prerequisites to Spiritual Awakening

Before I had my "spiritual awakening" in this way, I actually *had* engaged in some prerequisite behavior.

The easiest things to explain are things I've already written about. For example, in the year leading up to my spiritual Sight turning on, I massively increased my water intake. I was nursing my 1-year-old and pregnant with my second, and both of those activities made me super thirsty. So I was drinking water like crazy.

Also in the year preceding my awakening, I started daily breathwork. This was not done with any sort of conscious knowledge of breathwork. Instead, what happened was I realized that my muscles were very tight and I was having trouble relaxing my body, so I decided that every time I washed my hands, I would look in the mirror and breathe and consciously relax my shoulders. I tell this whole story at length with pictures in my class You Are A Healer, at allieduzettclasses.com. But I was doing daily breathwork and body relaxation—which together were oxygenating my body more than ever and serving my nervous system by relaxing my overly tight musculature.

Now, yoga.

I remember maybe being twelve when my dad taught me to use a search engine on the internet, and the first thing I searched for, as a little twelve-year-old, was information about YOGA.

I think my soul just knew that yoga was important to my life. So I was a little kid using the brand new internet to search for yoga instructions and my dad would print out the instructions for me, and every day through most of high school I did about an hour of yoga every day. In college, though, I fell off the yoga wagon and didn't really pick it back up again for years.

Before my awakening, I had been trying to get back into it and do some amount of yoga stretches every day. I had no idea at the time how strengthening and toning this was for my nervous system.

I was also a very diligent student of scripture—I always have been, since I was a child. As a kid I hated church but believed in God, and I prayed that God would make me like church and scriptures, and miraculously, He did. So even when I was a pre-teen I would study my scriptures and as a teenager, I had perfect seminary attendance and read scripture daily, often both morning and night. My favorite books to read in high school were commentaries on theology and doctrine. Before my spiritual awakening, I was very plugged into scripture study—and I do believe studying the words of wise people who are strongly connected to the Divine helps prime the soul for further personal revelation.

And, finally, I had a big call to *repent*—which, if you'll recall, literally means to "change the way you breathe." But for me, I had some "sins" to address and heal.

My Repentance Process

I always thought of myself as a pretty good person. I read my scriptures, honored my father and my mother, didn't lie or cheat or steal, and I abstained from alcohol, drugs, and other taboo foods and beverages of my religion. I've always had a heart for outcasts and I've worked hard to help the people in my life feel cared for. I really felt like spiritually, I had it made in the shade. I was pretty proud of that.

But I wasn't happy. Shortly before my spiritual awakening, I was feeling angry and bitter and resentful about the other people in my life who "weren't as good as me." Ha! Talk about self-righteousness. But I had the data. I told God: "Look. I read my scriptures, say my prayers, keep the commandments, and do the good things. And look at *these other people* in my life who aren't doing ANY OF IT!" And I was very accusatory and angry and I wanted God to do something about these "losers" in my life who weren't as good I was being.

I went to the temple over my concerns and my anger and bitterness. I wanted a miracle that would change the other people in my life.

So imagine my surprise and distress when God told me there, "Stop blaming the other people in your life. What if YOU are the problem here?"

I was sitting in the hall, waiting, and reading scriptures and praying about my problem, when I heard these words. I was stunned and angry. I told God, "What do you mean? I am doing EVERYTHING RIGHT!"

But I flipped open the scriptures and the pages landed on 1 Corinthians 11:11 (what a number!). This scripture is one in a passage about the different roles of men and women, and the message was that I was not living in spiritual alignment with my nature as a woman.

That entire temple visit was crazy. I kept asking God questions about what He was asking of me, and then I would flip my scriptures open. My scriptures would "randomly" open to 1 Peter 3:2, Genesis 2. Over and over, the message was clear: God was asking me to be more feminine.

I was livid. I remember saying, "Jeez! Being feminine isn't in the Ten Commandments, okay??!" And I felt very angry that God was telling me to be more feminine, because at the time I really felt like my core personality was very masculine. I was brash, aggressive, controlling, logical, strong. I felt like God was asking me to become a wimpy weakling and a delicate flower, and the idea of that just made me feel sick inside.

Also, I had no idea *how* to be feminine. The entire concept felt alien and terrifying and confusing. I didn't even know where to start.

But since God had asked me to do it, I decided I would do it.

Over the next few months, I was guided through a repentance process that felt like it nearly killed me. I would spend hours crying and feeling how unfair it was that I was a woman when I felt I really would have made a better man.

But I proactively started working on my issues, slowly learning to be more humble and vulnerable. I teach about the specifics in my class Heal Your Marriage, Heal YourSELF on allieduzettclasses.com. But the last part of myself I had to face was the part that felt that logic was supreme and intuition was not so good. In my research on feminine energy, one thing that kept coming up was the importance of intuition, and how "feminine intuition" is a core part of feminine energy. The sources I was reading often defined this as knowledge that came from mystical sources and that didn't make sense. The idea of trusting something that didn't make sense was terrifying to me—and yes, writing this out, I realize how silly it sounds, considering that I went on the whole journey in the first place because of psychically "hearing" the voice of God.

But still, even though I had experience listening to God and acting on spiritual promptings, the idea of prioritizing those was scary to me. The idea of having to choose between logic and intuition, and choosing the one that specifically *didn't make sense,* sounded totally horrible to me.

But I decided to be brave, and so one night I committed to God that I would live by intuition instead of logic, and that if any information came into my mind, I would believe it, and the weirder and more nonsensical it was, the stronger I would believe it and the quicker I would act on it. I told God, "This is on YOU now. Don't let me think of anything wrong!"

The next morning, just 5 hours later, I woke up early with a vision of someone's energy field. I knew exactly what was wrong in their body and was told mentally how to fix the problem. I was told to call this person up and go to their house and work on them with my hands and their energy field. I was terrified and put it off until ten in the morning, at which point I felt like God said, "You LITERALLY JUST PROMISED ME you would act on things that don't make sense! GO DO IT!"

So I went and visited with this woman I barely knew, did a healing technique I didn't really know, and actually solved the health problem. It was astonishing, and that was the day I really feel my third eye opened. After that, I was seeing people's energy fields and their health information everywhere I looked.

These days, I keep that ability turned off, like a lightswitch in my mind. I only turn it on when I'm being paid to do a session on someone, and I mention this because I don't like the idea of people thinking I'm just spying on their energy field all the time. I'm not.

One thing about this ability is—that it is physically demanding. Because, once again, the physical body is the vessel for spiritual information.

Which is why I feel so strongly that the first step in healing the ability to hear spiritual guidance is working on the physical body. This is what I did, even though I didn't realize I was doing it at the time. And this is what you will do, too, if you follow my recommendations in this book!

A lot of people get hung up on questions of trust, or beliefs that the Divine won't talk to them—and while those concerns are valid and important, they are things to worry about *after* the physical body is all caught up and *physically capable* of receiving spiritual connection.

Living in Alignment With Spiritual Blueprints

The issue of sex versus gender is very fraught right now. I'll just say that on an energetic level, the chakras of male people and female people are different. Masculine chakras emanate outwards; feminine chakras are vortexes pulling things inward. A person born with male genitalia typically has masculine chakras. The one exception I have seen was in an intersex woman, born with all possible genitalia (both male and female), but who identified as a woman and who indeed had feminine chakras. I have worked with numerous intersex clients and clients identifying as transgender, but in every case, their core chakra imprint was the one aligned most with their biological sex. I count biological sex this way: if you have primarily XY chromosomes, I would say you are male. If you have XX chromosomes, I would say you are female. If you have X0 chromosomes, I would say you are female. If you have XXY chromosomes, I would say you are what you sense that you are, but that you are probably female.

I do believe that for me, being able to reach the next level of spiritual insight was inextricably linked to me living in greater alignment with my spiritual blueprint as a female, as expressed by my DNA. You may or may not resonate with that yourself, and that is fine.

If you struggle to receive divine guidance and connect with your own intuition, and you also sense that you are not fully in alignment with a divine expression of your biological gender, I invite you to consider the possibility that you may need to do some work to live in greater alignment with your spiritual blueprint—even if, or especially if, you are not comfortable with the gender archetype your body corresponds with.

side is 90% whatever it is—with a small amount of the opposing force. These two energies create a polarity, where each one in its expansion births the other, and each in its contraction allows the other to shine.

This, to me, is the representation of a man being 90% in his masculine energy, with 10% of his spirit in divine feminine energy, and a woman being 90% in her feminine energy, with 10% of her spirit residing in internal masculine energy.

When I first started my journey with this, I was operating about 87% of the time from a masculine space—so basically my energy was inverted (my intuition gave me that number). People can invert their own energy; we can absolutely operate out of alignment with our spiritual biology, and most people really do. But getting into alignment with spiritual biology opens new doors that are not possible to work with otherwise.

There are several ways to be out of alignment with spiritual biology. The most obvious one is when a masculine force takes on excessive feminine characteristics, or a feminine force takes on excessive masculine characteristics.

But there are also healthy and unhealthy expressions of each form of energy. For example, the masculine force is designed to be proactive, taking decisive action. This is healthy—but if it crosses over into violent aggression, that is an unhealthy expression of masculine energy.

As a feminine example, feminine energy is naturally vulnerable—and to be clear, vulnerable is *not* a synonym for "weak." Emotional vulnerability, gentleness, and softness can be healthy expressions of feminine energy, but if that becomes a martyred victimhood attitude, that is an unhealthy expression of feminine energy.

And of course, masculine men can and should have that 10% vulnerable and emotional piece, and feminine women should have that 10% proactive, decisive piece. There is room for everyone to have access to all the healthy characteristics. It's just a matter of which characteristics are being expressed the most often. The expression of the characteristics is not referring to external behavior so much as internal processing and functioning. However, external behavior likely matches internal behavior. A woman who is outwardly expressing masculine energetic behavior is unlikely to have a strongly aligned feminine energy within. While the important thing is getting the internal energetic core in alignment, external behavior will tend to match the internal core.

A Brief Introduction to the Polarity

It's hard to understand masculine or feminine energy without the other there as a foil. The two energies define each other. It's hard to know what darkness is if you've never seen any light. The two energies define themselves in relation to each other.

And so, here are some explanations of the differences.

Where masculine energy is penetrative and emanating, feminine energy is absorbent and receptive. Consider the act of sex: this is a symbol of the male's penetrating energy and the female's receptive energy.

Where masculine energy is hot and bright, feminine energy is cold and dark. Consider the stereotype of the thermostat wars! Men want the air colder because their bodies literally run hotter, and women often feel cold and want the thermostat turned to be warmer.

Where feminine energy is ethereal and yielding, masculine energy is solid and unbending. Consider the bodies of men and women: the musculature of men is naturally harder and more unbending, whereas the body shapes of women are much more yielding and soft. Even men who don't exercise typically have stronger bodies than the majority of all grown women. Even women who exercise still tend to retain elements of softness to their physical bodies.

Where masculine energy is leading, feminine energy is following. This was a very distressing thing for me to come to terms with, because I view myself as a leader. When I prayed about it, I heard, "You are the left hand." I was making cookies at the time. I saw that my right hand, my dominant hand, was the masculine energy in this example: it was taking the lead with stirring. But my left hand was holding the bowl.

If I let go of the bowl, I couldn't stir. And if I tried to hold the bowl with my right hand and stir with my left, the stirring process was unnecessarily difficult and inconvenient. It made the most sense to let my right hand lead the process, and my left hand follow. This didn't mean my left hand was less important; both the masculine and feminine roles are equally important, just different in function and presentation. Being the follower is not "less than." It is just as important and perhaps even *more* important—because anyone can lead... but only if someone chooses to follow them. The follower gets to choose who they will follow, and if they do not volunteer their cooperation one way or another, the leadership will fail. The feminine "following" energy is *actually* the leading energy, in my opinion, because if the feminine energy decides not to cooperate with the masculine leadership, that masculine leadership is neutered and cannot move forward. By choosing who to follow and when to follow, the feminine energy enables masculine leadership. Without feminine enabling this way, masculine leadership is impossible.

Nature-wise, masculine energy is like the earth, and feminine energy is like water. The earth is steady, stable, solid. Water is always moving, always bringing life to wherever it goes. Without both earth and water, life cannot exist. You need both. One is not better or more important than the other.

Imagine two people holding hands and leaning back and running in a circle. The force of their opposition yet togetherness keeps them stable and steady. If one person lets go, or stops moving, or slugs along, it messes with the functionality of the pair. Each side has to lean into its opposing function to be steady and stable. But if they do lean into the opposing forces, the force there makes it so if one person lifts their feet off the floor, they can temporarily fly.

When a male force steps into masculine energy in a healthy way, and a female force steps into feminine energy in a healthy way, and they both lean into their opposing ends of the polarity, but hold hands with each other, it allows each person to take turns flying.

The Polarity Is Relative

It's important to remember that the expression of *yin* (feminine) and *yang* (masculine) energy falls along a spectrum.

- Children are *yang* to babies.
- Employees are *yin* to bosses.
- Bosses are *yang* to employees.
- All the people in the country are *yin* to the king.
- The king is *yang* to all the people in his country.
- The ladies-in-waiting are *yin* to the princess.
- The princess is *yang* to the ladies-in-waiting.
- Your dominant hand is *yang* to your non-dominant hand.

- Your non-dominant hand is *yin* to your dominant hand.

- Even our bodies are BOTH *yin* and *yang*.

Thus, the divine polarity of *yin* and *yang* is both situational and absolute. What this means is, we see these two forces in play daily, as we go through different circumstances that require us all to act in different *yin* and *yang* capacities. As an example, a mother is *yang* to her children, but *yin* to her husband. This is situational polarity. All relationships, including queer relationships, still operate on this spectrum, where one person will be more *yin* and one person will be more *yang*. And sometimes different circumstances require different expressions. For example, in a marriage relationship, a husband may be more *yang* and a wife more *yin* usually, but in a specific situation the wife may be required to take the lead and step into a more *yang* energy in that situation.

Yin and *yang* energies are also absolute. All people participate in this polarity and on a core soul level have a resonance more with one side than the other. The taijitu is NOT a picture of one person's soul that is 50-50 *yin-yang*; it is the picture of TWO souls who have full embraced their POLARITY. Each is 90-10. BECAUSE they polarize, they flow into each other and have the power to create all life.

Stepping into Healthy Expressions of Spiritual Biology

Again, this is a topic that could be explored for the length of an entire book, but my goal here is to give you a brief foundation so you can move on to some practical techniques for accessing your intuition and divine guidance.

I do believe that living in harmony with one's spiritual biology is critical to mastering spiritual insight. And this goes beyond the clothing you wear or the sports you enjoy. It's not so much about if you wear high heels or sneakers, or if you spend your free time knitting or riding a motorcycle, or if you typically cook dinner or mow the lawn. This is about spiritual alignment.

For men, here are a few ways you can step more fully into spiritual alignment with divine masculine energy:

1. Take action. The divine masculine is an active, proactive energy. What have you been procrastinating? Stop putting things off and get them done.

2. Exercise self-discipline. Unhealthy masculine energy seeks to control others, but healthy masculine energy controls itself. Where do you struggle with self-disclipline? Take some time to inventory your experience with self-discipline and start taking steps towards greater self-control.

3. Develop self-confidence. Masculine energy has a natural confidence, and stepping into that confidence with intention can be very powerful. It's worth it to work through your barriers to self-esteem. Often, self-confidence comes from self-respect.

4. Develop self-respect. Masculine energy is highly driven by a need for respect. Many men turn bitter because their needs for respect are not met by the women and others in their lives. But the secret to managing this is to develop *your own* self-respect. You develop your own self-respect by performing actions and accomplishing things that you are proud of. If you struggle with self-respect, it may be time to throw yourself into more proactive action with more self-discipline, so you can see results you have created yourself that you can be proud of, regardless of other people's opinions of you.

5. Engage in logic and analysis. Masculine energy is objective, logical, analytical. Emotions are important and worth honoring, but also, your masculine energy is designed to be more logical and objective. This is so you can be a force for wisdom when it comes to taking action. When there is a problem in your life, it's time to logically work through the behaviors you engaged in that brought you to that problem, so you can fix them.

6. Be a warrior. Masculine energy is designed to fight— in appropriate, divine ways. Ask the divine what you should be fighting for. Take care of your physical body and your mental and emotional sides in preparation for whatever conflicts you may be in charge of facing for your family.

7. Take care of your stewardship. Masculine energy is meant to provide the stuff of life for its dependents, such as a wife and children. What are you in charge of providing for? Are you doing a good job? Work with the divine to make a plan to do your best in managing your stewardship.

8. Start before you are ready. Masculine energy is a risk-taking energy. This does not mean you should jump into everything in your life without thinking first, but rather that sometimes to do the right thing, whatever that "right thing" is will require you to take action before you have all the answers. Where feminine energy is still, and can end up stagnant, masculine energy plows forward even when there aren't all the answers.

9. Stand up for yourself. Masculine energy has natural boundaries relating to control. Are you standing up for yourself or allowing other energies in your life to control you inappropriately? Masculine energy is a leadership energy. A book to consider reading is "Don't Let Her Lead" by Zak Roedde.

10. Heal your relationship with masculine energies in your life, particularly with your father. Healing your perception of fatherhood and masculine energy in a family setting can be healing not just for you, but for your entire family line forward and back.

11. Honor the feminine energies in your life. Remember that the emotions and intuition of the women in your life are just as valid as your logical and objective analysis.

For women, here are a few ways you can step more fully into spiritual alignment with divine feminine energy:

1. Practice *being*. Where masculine energy is about taking action and *doing*, feminine energy is about *being*. Try setting aside a few minutes a day to just exist, and nothing more. To *be* without worrying, without planning, without folding laundry or making dinner or thinking about who will take care of this or that. Going into a meditative space every day and just *being* is powerfully feminine. Relax and focus on your breathing.

2. Be open to receiving. Feminine energy is designed to receive. Where masculine energy is driven to provide, feminine energy needs to be willing to receive. Are you willing to receive?

3. Do something creative. The feminine energy is, at its core, an energy of birthing. It's not just about children,

it's about all creativity. If you don't have a creative hobby, try something out. You might take up watercolor painting, crochet or sewing, or some other creative pursuit. There are free tutorials for basically everything creative on YouTube. I love to write books as my creative pursuit. What can you create from your feminine energy?

4. Surround yourself with beauty. Masculine energy may provide the stuff of life, but feminine energy makes it beautiful and worth living for. What can you make beautiful in your life today? Feminine energy naturally is driven to beautify its surroundings and itself.

5. Be gentle—especially with yourself. Feminine energy can be the most spiteful and cruel of all energies; think of the wicked stepmother in fairy tales. It's not a coincidence that the bad guys in fairy tales are wicked stepmothers more than wicked stepfathers. Women can be uniquely cruel to others and to themselves. When you find yourself thinking cruel or bitter things, take a deep breath and reset; choose into gentleness instead. Choosing to see the best in people (without excusing abuse, of course) is a beautiful expression of feminine energy.

6. Connect with your physical body. Historically, feminine energy has been linked with embodiment because obviously, only female bodies can create other bodies. The feminine experience is unique in its

body-connectedness. Take time every day to check in with your body and to nurture it. Moisturizing, taking baths, doing breathwork, stretching and holding yoga postures, or anything else you can do to connect with your physical body in a restful, nourishing way is healing and feminine.

7. Be playful and spontaneous. Masculine energy is the one that's supposed to be doing the planning. The feminine energy *needs* time to just play and rest and do spontaneous things. This doesn't come naturally to all women, especially those who have not had a strong masculine force to rely on. But see if you can set aside some time specifically to do something spontaneous for yourself—every day, if you can.

8. Be vulnerable and honest about your emotions. Being emotionally vulnerable does not mean making yourself a martyr, blaming your emotions on other people, or being a "wimp." Emotional vulnerability requires taking responsibility for our emotions as well. Before you can be honest about your feelings with others, you need to understand them yourself. Journaling and engaging in regular self-reflection so you can fully understand your feelings is very feminine.

9. Connect with community. Masculine energy is independent, but feminine energy is interdependent and really benefits from social connection in a

different way than masculine energy does. I get most of my own social connection in my Facebook group, *Intuitive Healing with Allie Duzett*—but I try also to connect with my real life friends as often as possible. Visiting with other women and creating strong relationships with them is so nurturing and healing for feminine energy. If you don't know where to start, come make friends in my Facebook group.

10. Allow yourself to be led by your whims. Obviously you can't do this all the time, but the feminine energy needs to be able to just act on a whim sometimes. How can you be whimsical today? How can you take action on a thought or feeling that sounds fun or intriguing?

11. Honor the masculine energies in your life. If you have been controlling of masculine energies in your life, this is your call to step back and focus on nurturing your internal feminine energy, and encouraging the men in your life to step into their masculine leadership role in a healthy way.

Of course, stepping into your natural divine polarity does *not* leave any room for tolerating abuse from others. It is not possible to honor the divine polarity of those around us while playing along with abusive situations. Honoring other people does not mean not having boundaries.

Intuition and Your Marriage

You might have noticed that it can be really hard on a marriage when one participant starts engaging in rapid spiritual growth—and the other half doesn't. Or, shall we say, the other half doesn't *appear* to be growing at the same speed. This is a chapter about managing marriage during apparently mismatched spiritual growth periods.

Of course, this is a topic that can be a whole book in and of itself! But I wanted to just mention it quickly.

Again, it's controversial these days to talk specifically about heterosexual marriage, but that is what I am going to talk about here. Very often, it seems that women start becoming more spiritually active and aware far before their men do, and when this happens, their husbands can get very nervous or even angry and offensive or defensive. It is a tragedy when increasing spiritual connectively leads to a decrease in connection in marriage.

However, this is entirely avoidable.

The following is my opinion only and I encourage you to read it with the lens of your own intuition. We are all entitled to our own spiritual answers. But these are the things I feel impressed to share here.

First, every human is on their own spiritual journey. The idea that one person is growing faster than someone else on a spiritual level is just an erroneous perspective to me. The correct understanding is that every human is on their own journey, and that each individual's journey unfolds at exactly the right time and speed for them. If it feels like someone close to you is not growing quickly enough on a spiritual level, that is a **massive warning sign that you are the one in danger of hampering your own spiritual journey with judgment and erroneous perspective**. The enlightened thing to do is accept your spouse wherever they are on their spiritual journey (of course, this is not counting abuse—I'm talking about the run of the mill scenario where you take up meditation and breathwork and your spouse thinks you've gone insane).

When this happens, the first thing to do is start evaluating your own beliefs. For example, the belief that you are healing and growing faster than your spouse, or the belief that it's wrong for your spouse to experience exactly their own personal journey as *they* want to experience it (not how *you wish* your spouse would experience his or her own journey). Spiritual shifts can impact couples, but judgment, fear, blaming, and resentment should *not* come from our side. You are the one who has access to the true perspective, which is that everyone is on their own journey. It is a gift to you when your spouse experiences a journey on a different timetable from you. This gift allows you to practice finding peace and accepting others even when they do not understand you and even when you have a predisposition to be frustrated with their behavior.

Second, I feel very strongly that God is a smart guy and that He meant the Bible verses about husbands being in a position of authority over their wives. I know that is a triggering thing to hear for many people. It was very triggering for me. But in my own life, I do consider it my primary responsibility to submit to my husband. (Quick! Go scribble out your feelings about the word "submit!")

My husband opposed my work and my intuition from the beginning, and several years ago after hearing something in church, he told me to shut down my business and go "confess my sins" to our bishop. I was stunned, shocked, horrified, angry—I knew that I was doing the right things, and that he was in the wrong. But when I prayed about it, I felt like God told me that I still needed to submit to my husband.

So I shut down my business and went to the bishop in a spirit of honesty and humility.

The bishop said that the Holy Spirit confirmed to him the importance of my work, and he told me to tell my husband I needed to get back to work right away. That experience resolved so many of our conflicts—precisely because I did not conflict. My husband knows that if he ever asks me to stop doing my various things that I do, I absolutely will stop, because I honor the covenant I made to submit to him as he submits to God. The tricky thing that I used to always tell myself was: but what about when he's not listening to God? Then I get to do what I feel is right, right?

But what I feel like God told me is that I am not qualified to judge when my husband is listening to God or not. My job is to listen to God first and my husband second, and when I listen to God first, God tells me to listen to my husband.

I do feel that many women turn to spiritual practices as a way to get around submitting to their husbands, because it is scary and they don't know how to do it, and they don't trust the man they married to lead them with love and devotion and wisdom and care. But the only way husbands learn to lead is if we let them lead. We have to listen to them and act on what they say, and see what happens. The trick with submission is not just mindless and dangerous obedience; it's conscious, soul-guided choosing to be led—along with the **responsibility of sharing our authentic feelings as they arise, without blame or judgment.** This is the piece of the puzzle that I was missing for many years.

In a duality, one side must lead and the other side must follow. This is just a reality. It's the reality for your two hands as they stir a bowl of cookie dough. It's a reality for your two hands as they cut a piece of paper or write a letter. Those are symbols of a greater reality. One must lead, the other must follow. Following is not "less than." It is not "worse." It is not because women are stupider or unworthy of leadership.

I invite you to think of this in a different context. Consider the reality that the only way someone can lead is if someone else decides to follow.

In other words, the only thing that enables leadership is the wisdom and willingness of the follower.

The woman's role of "submission" is not so that women can be taken advantage of; it's so that they can experience deeply devoted leadership and tender care. When women fully respect and submit to their husbands, while also fully feeling their feelings and sharing those feelings as they arise, without blame or judgment, something magical happens. Suddenly, the man is empowered to take serious action—and he's not just empowered. He's also inspired by his woman and he is extremely careful in his leadership because he desperately does not want to hurt her. When a woman submits fully, while also sharing her feelings about what is going on as her feelings show up, she gets to **RELAX** and **REST**, and she also gets her feelings acknowledged and accounted for in the moment. A woman sharing her feelings honestly, openly, from a space of neutrality and not judgment allows the man to adjust his leadership to account for his feelings. When a woman does not share her feelings, this is not possible. But when a woman shares her feelings, the experience for both the man and a woman becomes powerfully responsive to the needs and desires of both partners. This is not about women being helpless or less-than; this is about women deserving to be cherished and taken care of, and to have her feelings cared for in a powerful way.

I know these are hard words, or at least they were hard for me and it has taken me years to understand them. For more information and practical information, I'll invite you to look up Zak Roedde on Amazon and read all three of his currently available books: *Irresistibly Feminine, Worthy Woman,* and *Don't Let Her Lead.* I would make all three books recommended reading for both men and women. They were life-changing for me and may be for you as well.

But in the context of the intuitive healing journey, this is what I would say to women.

Women, if your husband is skeptical or mean or scared of what you are doing, I would say to listen to that. If he tells you to stop doing something, I personally would stop and have stopped. I have very seriously put my money where my mouth is with this. However, the other half of the equation is to share how you feel, without blame or judgment.

When I say to share with your husband how you feel, I mean to literally speak about your literal feelings, inside of your own body. This is not the story, it's the feelings.

For example, yesterday, my spouse snapped at me on the way to church. I was upset and I started to cry—I cried all through church. I told myself all sorts of stories about how unfair it was that he treated me that way. I wanted to hide from him. I started shutting him out, not making eye contact, ignoring him. I prayed to God for help to be brave enough to fulfill my responsibility as a woman to share my feelings.

Eventually I was brave enough to go to him and say, "May I please have some help with my feelings?"

He said yes, and so I told him my feelings—and only my feelings. "I feel sad. I feel it in my core, in my gut. It feels swirling and heavy." And I just cried. Please notice that I did not share the story and I didn't blame him. I just told him the literal feelings as I was experiencing them. That is all I said. He held me while I cried. Eventually he said, "I'm sorry I snapped at you this morning."

When he said that, my body reacted and I shared that out loud. I said, "I feel a pressure in my chest and a lot of confusion and panic feelings." And I just kept crying. Did I tell him it was all his fault? No. Did I tell a story or explain why I felt that way? No.

Eventually I said, "I don't know why I'm crying so much!"

He said, "Well, I know why. You've had a rough day. The kids were up all night. You got almost no sleep. I snapped at you before church. You had to deal with the baby alone for hours in a high-stress situation. It makes sense and it is good for you to cry. And now you need to rest." And he pulled me to my feet and led me to bed, and stuck me in there for a nap.

That is a great example of how to vulnerably share FEELINGS in a way that resolves problems. Here I shared FEELINGS as I experienced them in the moment, without a story attached to them. He got to draw his own conclusions and take responsibility for his part to play in the creation of those feelings. And that inspired him to use his leadership to solve the two main problems here: my feelings and my sleeplessness.

Many times women feel they are sharing their feelings, when really they are sharing their stories, blaming, and judgments. Then they blame their men for not taking their "feelings" seriously, when what they were really giving to their men was not feelings at all, but blaming and judgment and stories.

We all know how terrible it is to have people come to us and tell us stories where we are the villains. It shuts anyone down and turns on natural, normal defense mechanisms.

Sharing actual feelings, as in pure straight emotions and physical body sensations shared from a space of observational neutrality, is a different thing altogether, and sharing those as a woman activates the defense mechanism in men the other way: your man will want to defend you.

Women: you will see shifts in your life as you start feeling your feelings in your body as you feel them, and as you share them with your husband in a way that is neutral and honest. Accepting your husband as he is and accepting his leadership as it is, but informing him of your honest, neutrally-reported feelings as you go, will change everything for you and heal you in a way you cannot even comprehend right now.

When you feel that your intuition is in direct contradiction with his decisions or input, your job is not to argue, your job is to share your feelings, as feelings. You don't say, "I think you're wrong." You ask permission to share your feelings ("May I share my feelings, please?"), because women sharing their vulnerable emotions is powerful and sharing them without permission is invasive. And when your man says yes, you express your feelings as you feel them. "I feel upset and I feel it in my guts. I feel tightness in my chest. I feel a pounding in my head." If he asks why, you don't say, "Because you are a jerk who isn't listening to me." Your feelings are about you, not him. You would say, "I feel upset because I feel like I got a clear spiritual answer, but I also know that we need to be on the same page for this answer to work out and I feel fearful and insecure thinking about the idea that I might be wrong, or that I might be right but unable to take action." Please notice how this is framed in a neutral, non-blaming way. If any blame comes up, it is so critical not to express it. Scribble it out, take it to God, but do not carry the energy of blame inside your heart when you are expressing your feelings. Blame is not a feeling; it's an attack.

For me, I have very powerful intuition, and on several occasions my spouse has opposed the decisions I wanted to make based on my intuition. When that has happened, I have deferred to him and seen blessings from it. I very strongly believe that listening to my husband this way only leads to blessings in the long term, even when it's hard in the short term.

My message to men is this: you are designated as the leader of your home. It is time to get very clear on your inner vision for your life and for your family. Your role is to lead with unwavering devotion. In the context of an apparently-uneven spiritual journey, your role is to lead your wife into her body when she is expressing discomfort with your spiritual journey.

What this looks like is: when your wife indicates in any way that she is uncomfortable with what you are doing, you ask her how this feels in her body. Use your leadership to lead her back to her feelings and where and how she feels them in her body when she gets caught up in her head and starts blaming, judging, or telling stories about what is happening. Help her resolve her feelings and physical body sensations using whatever tools strike you in the moment. As you hold space for her feelings and help her find healing, you will see how both of you leave the experience empowered and inspired, calmer, and more deeply bonded.

When we step fully into our divine polarity in the context of our marriage, leaving stories, judgments, and blaming alone, we can experience incredible healing both alone and together that is not possible any other way. When we step into our polarity in the context of our spiritual healing journeys, we find only peace and magnificent happiness, instead of conflict, blame, and strife. This is a reality that is possible for *you*.

Conclusion

In the next chapter, we're going to explore ways to connect with spiritual guidance. As we head into that, remember to consider the role of your spiritual biology in how you perceive spiritual information. Remember that your physical body needs for water, air, and nutrients need to be met in order for you to experience a bounty of divine insight.

Chapter 9

Alignment, Body and Spirit

All this talk of physical body care and getting into spiritual alignment with the physical body is critically important to having access to intuition and spiritual guidance. Since we experience spiritual guidance through the media of our bodies, we have to be taking good care of our bodies in order to be in a space where can reasonably expect easy access to answers.

However, it's not just our bodies that need to be in proper condition.

Any time we are out of alignment with Reality it mucks up our systems and makes it harder to see things or feel things clearly. If we want to be able to receive quality spiritual information, we need to be sure that on a spiritual level, we are living in alignment with Reality.

So let's talk about Reality.

When I talk about Reality, I am talking about things as they really, truly are: not how we want them to be, not how we perceive them to be, but things as they actually exist in this matrix called the Universe. To me, there is nothing more important than bringing ourselves into alignment with the nature of things as they really and truly are, and anything less than that leaves us living in problems. Why? Because when we are living out of alignment with how things really are, we are living in a space of delusion and failure. This is true in every instance.

To me, Reality is based on what I consider Universal Laws. I talk about these at length in my Intuition Accelerator program. But to me, Universal Laws include things like the Law of Cause and Effect, the Law of Compound Interest, the Law of Opposites. These Universal Laws dictate how everything in Reality shows up. One thing leads to another: cause and effect. The things we do consistently over time build up and compound in magnitude: compound interest. Everything shows up in a polarity or opposition: opposites. There are numerous Universal Laws and everything in the world runs on them, whether we like it or not.

However, even though these laws dictate how the world functions, we as individuals can rebel against the laws. This, to me, is the main reason why every major religion tends to have similar rules that relate back to these concepts. Stealing is commonly prohibited among many religions, and to me it's not just because "God said so;" rather, to me, "God said so"

BECAUSE stealing violates the Law of Cause and Effect and the Law of the Harvest, which states that "as ye sow, so shall ye reap." If one person plants the seeds and grows the crops, and another person steals those crops, the thief has unfairly inserted themselves into the divine cycle in play. They've intentionally disrupted one person from experiencing the fruits of their labor, and they will have to answer for that. They will start answering for it immediately in terms of their energy field getting gunked up, and they will answer for it in the long term in other ways.

Over time, everything balances out, and eventually the thief and the victim will both see their just rewards, whether in this life or a life beyond. That is my understanding.

But I bring this up because all of us live out of alignment with Reality from time to time, in one way or another. When we are dishonest, when we take something without compensating for it, when we are consumed with jealousy or negativity: these are all ways we use our agency, the power of choice, to live out of alignment with how the world really works.

To me, the Ten Commandments are a great shorthand for some of the specifics of laws we all do best to conform with. Thou shalt not kill, thou shalt not steal, thou shalt not bear false witness, thou shalt not covet—all of these things are specific rules that if we conform with them, we will be naturally living in greater alignment with the Laws of the Universe.

When we are out of alignment, it's hard to hear spiritual things clearly.

Once we've gotten our physical bodies in order, it's time to get our spiritual side in order.

Getting Your Spiritual Side In Order

What does it mean to get your spiritual side in order?

To me, it means identifying where you have been out of alignment with what is good and what is true and Real, and making restitution for those things, and realigning yourself with Reality.

What I recommend is to go year by year from your life, starting from maybe your mid-childhood or teen years, and write down anything you can think of that you did that was out of alignment, and that you never resolved. If you are religious, you might list this as your unresolved "sins," or just actions that you feel were wrong. This is the first of three lists.

As an example of things that could end up on this first list, as I was guiding a client through this exercise some years ago, up came an instance from when he was twelve years old, and he had lied to his mom about eating his dinner—he had instead thrown it into the trash. His body and energy field were still feeling guilty about this and he was 37. Obviously this was not a huge violation of natural law or something. No one died because he threw his dinner in the trash and told his mom otherwise. But because he had never resolved this situation, it was still bouncing around in his space and causing trouble.

So nothing is too small to catalogue and nothing is too big. We start just by writing down whatever comes to mind. You don't have to go year by year, either; you can just sit down and label your list "My Unresolved Stuff" and just write down whatever comes to your mind. That way, things will come to you in the order of priority to your soul.

But either way, you'll want to just prime yourself to be open to remembering the stuff you have done that was out of alignment. Things that were out of alignment could include:

- Lying
- Cheating
- Stealing
- Misleading others
- Acting out of feelings that you are better than other people
- Hurting other people either physically or emotionally
- Engaging in jealous feelings or behavior
- Acting out of anger
- Betraying others

I want to also mention sexual issues, even though those are controversial. The reason they are important to mention is because sexual energy is the foundational energy of the Universe, the energy of Life Itself. When sexual energy is channeled in certain ways, it violates the energy of the Reality.

The concept here is that things like using someone for sex, sexual abuse, and sexual infidelity are not just wrong because they are physically hurtful and harmful, and they are not just wrong because they hurt emotionally, but they are *also* wrong because all of those examples are demonstrations of grossly inappropriate use of the energy that is the source of all Life.

I will encourage you to study this out for yourself, in your mind and your heart, and come to your own conclusions. I am not going to levy any accusations against anyone or any behavior. You are capable of coming to your own conclusions about this topic. Some people view masturbation, pornography use, and "sleeping around" as inappropriate channels of one of the most serious foundational energies of the Universe. It could be argued that sexual energy should be reserved for relationships that are committed and that honor the foundationally important nature of this energy. These are things to consider as you look back over your sexual history to see if anything feels like it should be on this list.

Remember that situations where you were the victim do not belong on this list. That belongs on another list we will discuss later.

This first list is of mistakes you feel that you made that you need to make right.

Making Restitution

Expect your list of things to resolve to take a while to create and while to resolve. You won't do it all in one day—you do it a little bit at a time. But cataloguing what needs to be resolved and then taking one step at a time to address them can yield huge results, even if you go just a little bit at a time.

As you catalogue your past, some things will be easier to resolve than others. Sometimes "all" it will take to resolve something is a heartfelt apology—sometimes easier said than done! Sometimes you may need to pay for something, literally, financially. Sometimes it's not clear how to resolve something.

Heartfelt Apologies

I used to teach my little kids the following formula for apologies. When they hurt each other, they would have to say:

I'm sorry that I _____.

It was wrong because _____.

I won't do it again.

Please forgive me.

And I like that formula for apologies because it hits all the main criteria: it acknowledges the specifics of what was done wrong. Explaining *why* the action was wrong really drives home that the guilty party "gets it." And of course, a good apology also indicates that the person has learned from the situation and has committed to never do it again. And forgiveness—yes!

When we apologize, it can't be any of this general, "Whatever I did, I'm really sorry" business.

Some years ago, I had a yoga teacher who delighted in verbally abusing members of the class. She framed it as the "healing power of destruction" or some other such thing. During one yoga class, she spent the entire time calling out each student one at a time, and telling them all the flaws she could see about them. When she got to me, she spent the time roasting me for using a healing framework that *she* had taught to me. She had taught me how to assign numeric values to vibrations and compare them, and spent yoga class telling everyone how awful it was that I was using the technique so much. I was blown away, and frankly, my spirit went into shock. You just don't go to yoga class expecting your teacher to insult you and all your classmates publicly.

Years after this, that yoga teacher called me up. She said, "I need to move forward in my life, but God says I can't move forward until I ask for your forgiveness. Only I can't imagine *anything* I might have done to warrant that!"

I couldn't believe it.

I just said, "Of course I forgive you for anything that requires me forgiveness." And maybe I should have told her flat out that I considered her behavior that day to be emotionally abusive. But I didn't. And I am not sure that that yoga teacher fully benefitted from my forgiveness, not because I didn't forgive, but because she legitimately had no idea what she had done that was wrong.

We have to fully understand what we have done wrong in order to fully benefit from an apology and forgiveness.

From time to time I've seen on social media general pleas for forgiveness: "It has come to my attention that in the past I was not so great. I'm so sorry if I ever offended you. Please forgive me." I know these posts are well-meant, but I can't help but wonder if perhaps they are not as effective on an energetic level as actual real apologies for specific things.

Specific apologies are the most powerful sort of apologies.

Years ago, I deeply wounded my best friend, to the point that it irreversibly destroyed our friendship. I felt horrible. I didn't want to be the villain of our relationship, but in the moment I didn't know how else to behave. Perhaps you can relate.

The very *idea* of verbally connecting with that friend ever again was terrifying to me. But every day I knew I had done the wrong thing, and I obsessed over it for years.

Several years into doing this to my friend, I heard a podcast from someone who I will never remember. They said to try apologizing this way: to call up the person you wronged, and use the following script:

> Hey, it's _____, and I know we haven't talked in a while and I know it's because I hurt you, and you don't have to say anything—I'm just calling to apologize. I'm so sorry for _____. It has weighed on me so much. I am so deeply sorry. I know what I did was wrong. I hope that you can forgive me, but even if you can't, I just wanted you to know that I am so sorry and I hope you are living your best life. Have an incredible day.

And then you just hang up!

I paraphrased the script, but hearing that recommendation on that podcast really struck me, and I decided to give it a try. It took me some time to gather my courage, but I called up my friend and called her up, and told her my apology and hung right on up afterwards, and then I cried and cried but felt so much better. So I will recommend this technique to you if it feels right.

The happy ending is that a year later or so, that friend emailed me to say thank you for that apology, and to confess that *she* had been devastated when I hung up, because she wanted so badly to apologize to *me*, too. We're not close or anything, but I think on both our ends we feel that the energy of that horrible time in our lives has been resolved.

It is absolutely worth it to apologize to the people you have wronged, and to do it in a specific way.

When You Can't Apologize

Sometimes you can't apologize, for whatever reason. Sometimes the person you wronged is literally dead and you can't exactly call them up on the phone. Sometimes it's a person who seems to have dropped off the face of the earth; you just can't track them down. Sometimes you might need to issue an apology to someone who is unsafe to contact for one reason or another—for example, an narcissistic ex-boyfriend or something that maybe you still wronged in some way.

When you cannot apologize, I recommend doing a spirit-to-spirit conversation.

You start by imagining the other person as realistically as possible. I often do this in my car, and imagine the other person in the passenger seat. From there, you talk to them as if they are really there, "spirit to spirit."

Part of the power of "spirit to spirit" conversations is imagining the other person's response. Sometimes they will "respond" to you in your mind, and their responses can be very enlightening. Sometimes no matter how much you apologize, the imagined responses will never be positive and accepting—and that is okay. You don't need them to forgive you, you just need to do what you can on your end to heal the situation. The rest is up to them.

Sometimes when you do a spirit to spirit conversation, you cannot even imagine the other person listening. What this feels like is, you try to imagine the other person coming to sit with you and talk, and even in your imagination, they are too angry to come any closer to you, and they reject the imagined discussion entirely.

When this happens, I recommend "writing" your apology in an imaginary letter—just speak it out loud or in your mind and imagine the energy of the apology being placed in a letter—and then send that letter to the person's imaginary "waiting room," for them to read and accept or reject on their timeline.

You may find that spirit to spirit conversations and apologies can be truly life changing.

You can also use this technique just to have hard conversations with people in your life that real conversations are "too hard" with. For example, if you are struggling with your spouse, but you know he would not handle your concerns well, you could express your concerns to his *imagined* self in the passenger seat of the car, and imagine *his* responses back to you, and have the conversation that way. I have seen many miracles with spirit to spirit conversations that lead to real life results and changes.

If you know you owe someone an apology, and you *could* technically apologize to them in real life but that sounds too hard, doing a spirit to spirit conversation can be a good stopgap. You start with the spirit to spirit conversation, and ask the other person when it would be best to apologize in real life. What do they say? Take note of their answer and use it to inform your real life apology.

Financial Restitution

When I was a teen, I once cheated my employer. I justified it at the time. I was being paid $7 per hour but I would charge my employer for the time it took me to actually walk to work every day—about a $1 extra charge each way. At the time I didn't feel bad about it, but years later, this situation cropped up on my own list of things I needed to make right.

The next time I was in town, I went to that employer—who did not remember me at all, I might add—and I explained the situation and that I wanted to make it right. He asked how much I owed. The answer was about $25. He told me to donate that amount somewhere and call it good, so I did—even though in my total account at the time there was just about $70. It was still a leap of faith for me at the time, just because I was so broke, but sending off that $25 check felt so good. It felt amazing to have that situation resolved.

Financial restitution is extremely freeing, and you won't know how freeing it is until you try it for yourself.

Some years ago, while I was on a road trip, I got an unexpected text from an unknown number. This person introduced herself as a client that I'd had in the olden days, back when I did sessions first and *then* required payment. She had never paid for the session I completed for her, and she felt horrible about it. She felt like she was trapped in her life, and she said that when she prayed about why she couldn't move forward, the answer was that she had stolen that work from me and never compensated me for it. She felt that to get right with the Divine she needed to pay what she owed.

Only, there was one problem: she owed me $150 for the session, and she only had $160 in her account.

Nowadays I require payment before I do a session, but back then, I would do the sessions first, and fairly regularly people just wouldn't pay. Once a year I would go through my outstanding invoices and proactively forgive them. I would cancel the invoice on my end, and then email the person directly and explain that their bill had been forgiven. This forgiveness process wasn't always easy—it felt like I had been stolen from and I had barely any money myself, which made it extra hard to let go of money people owed to me—but I did feel better after it was complete.

So I had already forgiven this session formally a long time before, but the fact that I forgave didn't matter for this woman's personal growth. It wasn't enough to be forgiven, she *also* needed to do what was right on her end.

That story ended tragically: she ended up sending some fraction of the amount, and then was too afraid to send the rest because she didn't believe that God would come through for her if she made things right financially when she had so little money. I hope that things are going well for her now. For me, I fully believe that when we make things all the way right, even if it drains our resources, we are taken care of positively as a result.

Making financial restitution is in one way a very difficult thing to do, particularly if you have no money. I fully get this and have been poor for a lot of my life. It's hard when you're broke and you know that you owe money to make a situation right.

However, this is also one of the easiest ways to make restitution. Just sending a check can sometimes make things right, right away. If you have intentionally or accidentally cheated someone financially, I urge you to take the leap of faith necessary to make it right—even if you feel like you do not have enough. See how the Universe and the Divine pull through for you.

Tithing

I'll mention here that I do believe tithing is a Law of the Universe (yes, capitalized!). This is the principle of giving back ten percent of your increase to our Source. Your intention is supreme here.

I tithe to my church, but many people tithe to other charity organizations. You can tithe in a way that you feel is acceptable to the Divine.

Last year, something happened in my church that left me feeling uncomfortable with how my tithing funds were being spent. I asked the Divine in prayer if it would be okay to donate my tithing to my favorite charity instead. I felt to open my scriptures, and I "happened" to open directly to the scripture in Malachi that says to bring the tithes to the Lord's storehouse. So I felt that for me, even though I may disagree with how my church always spends the money that I donate, for now donating to my church is the right choice for me.

It's important that you feel the approval stamp of the Divine on your choice to where to tithe, wherever that is for you.

I will mention that I feel that tithing financially is critical. I know sometimes people will tithe by offering free sessions, for example, doing one free session out of every 10 sessions. I have not met anyone financially stable who at least has claimed to do this. I personally believe that no amount of tithing sessions directly or work directly can replace actual financial tithing. But I invite you to experiment with this yourself.

Sometimes tithing and charitable donations, when done with intention, can help make restitution for unrelated issues from your past. If there is someone you have wronged or if there is something you have done that was wrong that is not easy to fix, sometimes this is a way that the issue can be remedied. For example, say you engaged in self-harm at one point. How do you make restitution for that? You might engage in greater self-care, or you might consider making a financial donation to an organization that helps prevent self-harm or treat those who are self-harming. Just something to consider.

Trauma and Mistakes

One thing I want to mention is the difference between mistakes you need to make restitution for and things we just *think* we need to apologize for. A lot of times abuse survivors, for example, will repeatedly ask God for forgiveness, but not feel it—not because God doesn't care, but because there's nothing for God to forgive in the case of abuse. The problem isn't that God doesn't care, it's that the survivor is asking for the wrong manifestation of God's love.

Sometimes something terrible has happened in our lives, and it needs to be resolved, but it was *not* our fault and therefore apologizing won't help. It will be wise to really sit with the situations of your life and make an objective determination of what was "your fault" and what was not "your fault." When you try to make restitution for situations where you were the victim, you will fail, because no restitution was necessary in the first place.

When Things Cannot Be Fixed

What about when things cannot be fixed? We may all have situations that went dreadfully wrong and now it feels like there's nothing to be done.

I would just invite you to consider using your intentions to come up with an alternate solution. Like in my example earlier of cheating my employer of $25—he had me donate the money to an institution and called it good.

Doing service for others with the intention of repairing the bad energy incurred from whatever happened in the past can be a good option. Donating money with the same intention can be good. I know that part of this book is about the struggle to hear spiritual guidance, but you *can* ask for spiritual guidance on ways to make restitution for events where it seems there is no good or clear way to fix things.

Sometimes you *can't* fix things, and that's okay. The most important thing is healing your own energy field, your own spiritual energy, that is keeping a balance of what you are putting out into the world. If all you can do is fix something on your end, emotionally, that is critical.

The Forgiveness List

Speaking of fixing things on your end, let's talk about forgiveness. Hopefully you started your first list, of things you did wrong that need to be made right. The second list is of people and situations that you need to forgive.

On this list, you'll write down everything people have done to you or to people you care about that you are still angry about, that you haven't forgiven.

I'm talking your ex-boyfriend, the best friend in high school that told your secret to whoever, your mom and dad, your teacher that embarrassed you in class. I'm talking your spouse, your children, your boss. But I'm also talking the government, your local political leaders, any religious leaders you take issue with, and basically the bigger picture as well. Is there a political party you need to forgive? A political leader you need to forgive?

Take some time and write down the situations you need to forgive. It's hard to feel spiritual guidance when our bodies are filled up with unforgiveness. We need to make things right where we have wronged others, *and* we need to forgive others who have wronged us. This clears up emotional space and lightens the load on our nervous systems so we can more easily hear the voice of our own intuition and the Divine.

How to Forgive

Some years ago, I was reading in a text called the Book of Enos, where the titular character is forgiven for his sins and asks the Divine, "Lord, how is it done?"

I read that as: "Lord, how is forgiveness done?"

And I asked to please see the forgiveness process myself.

What I saw was black tornados of unforgiveness clogging up a person's physical body. I saw that forgiveness dissipates those tornados and restores peace where there was previously turbulence. I saw that while "forgiving" can be kind of nebulous, if you actually go in your mind and imagine this process, you will see for yourself how if you can imagine the turbulent tornado of unforgiveness and just breathe it out, transforming it from a tornado to ashes that you exhale out of your system, you *will* feel better.

To me, the act of forgiveness is energy medicine. It is the transmutation of turbulence into calm. If you can take the turbulent feelings about the issue you haven't forgiven, and transition it into calm, you can feel peace.

As you go down your forgiveness list and start working through it, this is an excellent exercise to try. With each person, imagine gathering up all the turbulence you can find in yourself into one big tornado. Then take a deep breath and imagine it breaking down into dust and leaving your system with your exhale. If you can't visualize it, that's fine. Just think about what it would be like if all the unforgiveness toward this person were a tornado that you breathed out of your system. See how this can create a shift in your space.

You can also try using the scribbling technique (covered in a later chapter) to remove the turbulent energy of unforgiveness from your physical body.

Additionally, here are some tapping scripts to help you as you go through this forgiveness process. Tap on your forehead or collarbone and say aloud three times each:

- Even though I don't remember all the things I haven't forgiven, my memory is bringing the instances back to me in the perfect timing.

- Even though I don't know how to forgive in every instance, I am figuring out how to thoroughly forgive a little more every day.

- Some people forgive each other.

- It could be safe for some people to forgive each other.

- It might be safe for me to be forgiven.

- It might be safe for other people to forgive me.

- Even though I don't believe I deserve to forgive, I deeply and completely love and accept myself.

- It might be safe to believe I deserve to forgive.

- What would it feel like if I could forgive myself?

- Maybe I could consider forgiving myself.

- What if I forgave myself?

- What if I forgave others?

- What if it could be safe for me to forgive others?

- What if I knew that forgiving others didn't make what they did okay?

- What if I knew that when I forgive, it doesn't excuse the other person's behavior?

- It could be safe to forgive, because there is always a divine record kept of the other person's behavior.

- I can forgive and release the record of my distress from my physical body.

- It could be safe for me to forgive myself and others.

- Even though I don't know how I am forgiving people I never thought I could forgive, I find myself suddenly able to start forgiving them.

- Even though I have never known how to forgive myself, I find myself suddenly willing and able to forgive myself.

- Forgiveness can be safe and beautiful.

- I can deserve forgiveness.

- I can deserve to forgive.

- I can forgive.

- I forgive.

One note here is that of course, forgiving someone *just* means releasing the turbulence from your own heart. It does *not* make what that person did okay. It does not excuse them for what they did. It excuses *your body* from being the record-keeper of what they did.

Everything you forgive just ends up in "the great evidence room in the sky." Basically, the Divine is keeping a record of everything you have suffered. It is safe to forgive even the worst offenders, and know that the Divine will not allow them to escape the justice that is required. You don't have to use your physical body as the proof of other people's cruelty. It is safe to release your body from that bondage of unforgiveness. Forgiving just takes the burden of other people's bad choices away from your body, and turns it over to the Divine so that something can be done about it.

It is safe to forgive.

I want to also add that sometimes forgiveness must be done over and over and over again. I had a horrible experience where I was betrayed and my betrayer actually vandalized my living space, so every time I walked into a certain room, I was reminded of what they had done. It was hugely distressing to my system.

Even after I discovered this forgiveness technique, I would breathe out the dark tornadoes of my unforgiveness, only to have them re-form and come back—sometimes instantly or within minutes.

To me, this is an example of why anyone would have to forgive "seventy times seven" times. Sometimes an offense feels so egregious to your system, you need to forgive it over and over and over again—and that is okay. Just keep going. Seventy times seven times. You can do it. Don't keep score. Just breathe out the tornadoes.

One more note about this is that when those tornadoes keep re-forming, a lot of times it is due to underlying belief patterns that need to shift. For example, in my story, I had beliefs like, "My betrayer doesn't deserve to be forgiven for what they did," and "You can't just forgive vandalism."

You can use your logical thinking brain to reason out what underlying beliefs you might have that make it hard to forgive, such as "No one should have to forgive their own mother" or "It is wrong to forgive something so egregious." You can also try feeling out whatever beliefs there might be. Just make them up and write them down.

Then rewrite them. If you had the belief that "My betrayer doesn't deserve to be forgiven," the rewritten belief could be, "Even my betrayer is a divine eternal being who deserves forgiveness based on that alone," or perhaps, "Even though my betrayer may not deserve forgiveness, I deserve the freedom of forgiveness." You can tap in the new beliefs by stating them out loud while tapping on your forehead or collarbone. It may take a few times, or more than a few times, to tap them in. But this may help you shift into a space of forgiveness.

Anywhere you can move into a space of forgiveness, you will see that your body loosens up, you feel mentally and physically and emotionally clearer and healthier, and most importantly—you will see how that openness facilitates a greater ease with divine and intuitive information.

The Third List: Your Trauma and Victimhood

The first list was a list of things you've done wrong, and the second list was a list of things you need to forgive. This third list is of your unresolved trauma and the ways in which you have been victimized—and where you still feel victimized.

I realize this has potential to be a long list—just like the other lists! The important thing is just to get it started. All of these lists are things you will add to and work through for your whole life. This is how to stay on top of your life. You create these inventories that help you take care of your mistakes, forgive those who have wronged you, and heal from your trauma.

Where have you been victimized? Where have you been wounded and have never fully healed it?

The things on this list could be quite varied. Of course abuse of any kind would be on this list, as well as unkind words that echo in your mind from past conversations, times you've been embarrassed, the hard stuff from your life. Write down the specific instances. The time that X happened, the time that Y happened.

This will be emphatically not fun. This exercise isn't supposed to be fun. This exercise is to help you figure out what issues you need to prioritize clearing so that your emotional energy and physical energy is no longer devoted to managing the emotional residue of these situations.

Once you have created your list, you job is to pick just one thing and start working on it. I have a huge repository of sessions, many available by donation, on my website, allieduzettclasses.com. You can listen to these sessions while doing the dishes, folding you laundry, going on a run, or driving around in your car—they can fit into your life and help you clear out and heal old trauma.

Additionally, you can use inspired journaling, scribbling, or my favorite self-healing technique to help clear out and heal from these old traumas as well, and all of these techniques are explained in the upcoming chapters. This is because these techniques aren't just great for helping you heal from your emotional trauma; they're *also* great at helping you discern spiritual information.

This list has the potential to be overwhelming, but I am telling you now: there is no reason to be overwhelmed. We just work on one thing at a time and clear them out. You are reading this book. You are taking action. You are working through your stuff. You are doing it. So there is no reason for despair or impatience or overwhelm; just doing a little bit at a time, over time, adds up. It's the Law of Compound Interest. If you take a little bit of action on your healing every day, it will add up and compound to be greater than the sum of everything you have done. You will see for yourself how your little daily efforts snowball over time.

The Bonus List

One more list you might consider making is a list of all the things you need to accomplish, but haven't. Yes: a to-do list. This list would especially include things you have started but never finished.

Having unfinished business really does weigh on a spirit, and it can weigh on *your* spirit.

If you find it difficult to focus and feel clear-minded, often that can be linked to the emotional and energetic weight of unfinished business. Making a list of the things in your life that are incomplete, and then systematically completing them, can free up space in your mind and in your spirit so that you have the capacity to notice subtler things.

Conclusion

It is critical to clear out any misalignments in your energy field and spirit that have resulted from things you've done wrong, from unforgiveness, and from things others have done wrong to you. Keep reading to learn more tools to deal with these things—but don't forget to take the time to create these written inventories and start working through them. You will see for yourself how taking action in this way changes and heals your life.

Chapter 10

Four Keys to Success

You've learned a lot of things that go into being able and ready to receive divine insight! I was about to pronounce this book complete, but realized that I needed to go back and add in this chapter on four additional keys to success. These concepts are very important and this is where I need to mention them.

In addition to everything else you've learned so far, these are four more keys to success. They are:

1. Grounding
2. Polarity
3. Calling back your personal power
4. Knowing you deserve access to intuitive information

These four concepts may be familiar to you because they are my four foundational sessions on allieduzettclasses.com. I always recommend that people do Resetting Polarity, Calling Back Your Personal Power, You Deserve To Heal, and the

Grounding Session before they do *any other healing work whatsoever*, because these concepts are so critical to success in healing. I strongly, strongly recommend heading over to my website and working through those sessions as soon as possible. In the meantime, I'm going to explain what these things each mean and how to work with them on your own.

Grounding

You might have heard of being "grounded" before. I'm not talking about when your mom says you have to stay in your room until dinner; I'm talking about the kind of grounding yoga teachers make you do.

This kind of grounding refers to connection. It means that your body is fully connected to your spirit, and your body and spirit are both connected to the earth and to the heavens. When you are fully connected in this way, you are grounded.

Most people are not grounded, for any number of reasons person to person. Most of the time the reason is trauma. Any kind of emotional or physical trauma can cause a person to become ungrounded, and then it typically takes some amount of work to get grounded again. Car accidents and sexual abuse in particular get people to come ungrounded, as well as things like public humiliation and other sorts of big traumas.

You may be ungrounded if:

- You have trouble identifying when you are feeling feelings
- You have trouble falling asleep
- You have trouble staying asleep
- You don't feel connected with your body
- You don't feel connected to God or the earth itself
- You have a sense reading this that you are ungrounded

In my Grounding Session, I reset your grounding so that you are grounded again. That is the easiest way to get grounded: have a qualified person clear out the trauma that caused you to become ungrounded and then reset your system so you are grounded again. But other things you can do to help yourself get grounded include:

- Spending time in nature, especially barefoot
- Buying and using grounding mats (look for them online)
- Washing your hands mindfully
- Any kind of mindfulness that draws your spiritual focus to the inside of your body
- Eagle Pose in yoga

You know that you are fully grounded because you will feel very calm and at peace being inside your own body. You feel your feelings as they come up. You feel connected to yourself.

You fall asleep much more easily. When you ask yourself if you are grounded, you feel a sense of *"yes, I am grounded."*

Being grounded is very stabilizing to the spirit. Being grounded is an extra layer of protection against spiritual destabilization. Often when people *do* receive answers but don't feel that they can trust those answers, it's because they were ungrounded when they received those answers. Being ungrounded doesn't prevent spiritual information from coming to a person, but it does increase the likelihood that the spiritual information will not be entirely accurate or trustworthy, and that the person who is ungrounded will have a harder time discerning what is true and what is not true. Being grounded allows you to much more easily trust that you are receiving accurate information.

This is not a book about muscle testing, but if you are familiar with the concept of muscle testing, I'll just add that it is impossible to receive accurate answers to muscle testing if you are ungrounded. Being grounded is essential to muscle test accuracy.

Here are some tapping scripts related to grounding. To use them, please tap on your collarbone and say each script aloud at least three times. These are scripts you can copy down and use daily as needed.

Tapping Scripts

1. Some people are safe when they are fully grounded.

2. It could be safe to be fully grounded.

3. I could accept divine assistance in becoming grounded.

4. I can choose to be grounded.

5. I choose to be grounded.

6. I invite my spirit and my body to experience as full a connection as is safe for me at this time.

7. Every day my body and spirit get safer and safer to be fully connected.

8. My left brain and right brain could be safe to connect.

9. I choose into fuller connection between my left and right brain, my body and spirit, and my Self and the Earth.

10. It can be safe to be grounded.

Put your hands on your heart and breathe it in. Imagine your spirit fully inside your body, with your spirit feet inside your physical feet, your spirit hands inside your physical hands, your spirit torso inside your physical torso, your spirit head inside your physical head. Imagine a hat appearing on your head that helps keep your spirit safely within your body, if that feels appropriate and safe. Breathe it in.

Polarity

I mentioned earlier that all humans are electric. We all run on electricity. Electricity, like magnetism, deals with poles: positive and negative. Just like a magnet, all human beings have polarity. Ideally, all of us are electrically north-south polar, but just like with grounding, trauma can mess with the system. Very often, people's electric fields are not north-south polar, but south-north polar, east-west polar, or west-east polar. Sometimes I will see people whose polarity is so off that it can't even stay still at all; their polarity just swings back and forth.

When your polarity is off, you will get inaccurate answers. "Yes" will feel like "no," and vice versa. It becomes very hard to trust yourself because your polarity is off.

I have a Resetting Polarity session on allieduzettclasses.com, but additionally, something you can do is tell yourself out loud, "I am north-south polar!" as often as feels appropriate, and imagine an arrow inside of your head pointing forward, between your eyes. This might not sound very helpful but it really can be. Very often when people imagine that arrow inside their heads pointing off-center, and then they imagine bringing that arrow to a forward-pointing direction, they can feel very, very different. Please see for yourself!

When polarity is off, it is very difficult to be accurate with intuitive information. Resetting your own polarity and making sure your system is north-south polar can make it much easier to receive intuitive answers.

Here are some tapping scripts related to grounding. To use them, please tap on your collarbone and say each script aloud at least three times. These are scripts you can copy down and use daily as needed.

Tapping Scripts

1. Some people can be north-south polar.

2. It could be safe for me to be north-south polar.

3. I can choose to be north-south polar.

4. I am north-south polar.

Imagine that arrow in your brain pointing forward, between your eyes. Imagine light solidifying it into place there. Breathe it in.

Calling Back Your Personal Power

Everyone is born with personal power: your personal agency, or power of choice. Sometimes, though, we consciously or unconsciously give some of this power away. You know you have given your personal power away whenever it feels like you HAVE to do things for others, or when you feel like you have no choices, or when you feel controlled or like your emotions don't matter.

If you struggle with appropriate boundaries, a lot of times that is because of issues with your own personal power.

What lost personal power feels like:

- No or insufficient boundaries
- Getting walked on
- Not feeling like "yourself"
- Feeling "lost"
- Not sure what you're doing in life
- Feeling like everything in your life is beyond your control
- Feeling like you have to submit to other people's needs and wants and desires ahead of your own

What regained personal power feels like:

- Feeling completely in charge of what you are doing
- Taking responsibility for ALL of your choices
- Being able to say NO and YES when you want to
- Living without guilt and shame
- Feeling solidly associated with your own body
- Inner knowingness of Self

If your power has been given away to others in the past, of course you will struggle to receive intuitive answers. How can you receive intuitive answers when your personal power to do so is gone or diluted among other people?

I have a whole session designed to call back your personal power for you, but something you can do for yourself is to go in your mind and imagine your personal power spread out among many people, anyone you might have given it to. And then just call it back. Imagine it leaving all those other people and places. Wash it off from any yucky energies and breathe your power back in.

The time is now to step into your power and be who you are meant to be and do what you are meant to do.

You do not owe anyone else your personal power.

You always have the power to choose.

You are responsible for yourself and not for other people. You are responsible for your own power and no one else is responsible for that. It is safe to call back your personal power and experience it for yourself. You will see for yourself how if you have struggled to receive answers in the past, having your own personal power back with you can make a big difference.

Here are some tapping scripts related to your personal power. To use them, please tap on your collarbone and say each script aloud at least three times. These are scripts you can copy down and use daily as needed.

Tapping Scripts

1. It could be safe to call back my personal power.

2. I choose to have all my personal power back with me, where it belongs.

3. It is easy for me to contain, retain, and maintain my own personal power.

4. My personal power is mine.

5. I accept my own personal power.

6. My personal power returns to me clean and bright and ready to be mine again.

7. I forgive those who I feel took my personal power.

8. I choose peace when I think about my personal power.

9. I feel my personal power within me.

10. I accept the personal power within me.

Imagine your personal power as a color. What color is it? Imagine scanning the entire planet for traces of it that have been scattered about. Imagine calling them all back to you. See the colors come racing back, see them washed clean, and then see them rejoin you once again.

You Deserve The Answers You Seek

Do you truly know that you deserve to receive answers?

Or is there a part of you that still feels unworthy? Or that might actually even enjoy living in confusion?

It is critical that you fully believe that you deserve answers.

My session called You Deserve To Heal is all about helping the subconscious mind accept healing in general, but when it comes to receiving answers, we specifically need to believe we are worthy of receiving answers. Here are some tapping scripts related to feeling worthy of receiving answers. To use them, please tap on your collarbone and say each script aloud at least three times. These are scripts you can copy down and use daily as needed.

Tapping Scripts

1. It could be safe for me to receive divine clarity.

2. It could be safe for me to receive spiritual answers in a way that I easily understand.

3. I easily understand the answers I receive to my spiritual questions.

4. Answers flow to me as soon as I ask my questions.

5. I choose now to release any blocks I have against receiving answers.

6. I choose now to release any blocks I have against feeling deserving of receiving answers.

7. I choose to believe in my own worthiness to receive answers.

8. I am good enough to receive answers.

9. I am good enough to experience powerful, accurate intuition.

10. I deserve to experience powerful, accurate intuition.

11. I now accept a divine gift of powerful, accurate intuition.

12. I forgive myself for past instances where I felt misled or betrayed by my intuition.

13. I forgive God and my body for the times I felt led astray by the answers I thought they gave me.

14. I choose a new way of living, in trust of intuition.

15. I believe in my own worthiness to receive divine answers.

16. I know that God wants me to receive answers.

17. I know that my body wants me to receive answers.

18. I know that my own spirit wants me to receive answers.

19. I choose to believe in my own deservingness.

20. I deserve to receive powerful, accurate spiritual answers to the questions I ask.

Put your hands on your heart and breathe it in.

Conclusion

Being fully grounded and properly polarized is critical to your intuitive ability—and so is having all your personal power with you. Knowing on a soul level that you deserve to receive answers is also key.

Chapter 11

Beginning to Receive

The first step to getting more spiritually in tune is focusing on the physical body—because if the physical body is dealing with chronic shallow breathing, chronic dehydration, insufficient nutrition, toxic buildup, or nerve weakness, it's going to be almost impossible to have a good spiritual connection.

The physical body is the vessel for receiving spiritual guidance. We perceive spiritual information with our nerves, and those sensations become thoughts in our brains—literal items made of neurons and atoms. So it is critical to address physical body issues first.

We also have to address our spiritual misalignments. We make things right where we have messed up; we forgive others when others have hurt us or ourselves when we have hurt others or ourselves; and we work on healing our emotional trauma.

But once those issues have been addressed, or at least been started, it's time to get into the meat of recognizing spiritual information and how to use it.

When You're Not Used to Receiving Answers

Some of my readers say they *never* feel answers to their prayers, or they *never* feel connected with their intuition. The first step for those people is, again, working through everything in the earlier chapters—but once those things have been addressed, we have to talk about what it means to receive answers.

When you're not used to receiving answers, often the first thing you need to do is **revise your expectations**. Divine and intuitive insight come softly, subtly, almost as if on the breath of your imagination. It is rare for insights to come clearly and with force. If that is what you are expecting—clear, obvious, in-your-face directives that are as easy to discern as words on your iPhone screen—that is not a realistic expectation.

This is why it's so important to strengthen your physical body and remove the spiritual clutter from your soul. What you are seeking is something so ethereal and soft, it will be very difficult to sense if you are distracted by your own unforgiveness or despair or past abuse or past mistakes.

As you prepare to experience greater intuitive insight, know that you are *not* looking for grand insights that come obviously and unmistakably. You are opening yourself to the quiet things, the whisperings, the soft hints that your nervous system picks up on with the gentleness of a butterfly. You are looking for quiet things, not loud things.

In my opinion, the problem was never that you weren't getting answers—the problem was that your system was too cluttered and unsupported to hear and recognize the answers.

Now that you are actively supporting your physical body and working through your spiritual clutter, it will get easier to pick up on the subtle things.

I know that one common worry is about receiving spiritual information, and not knowing whether or not it can be trusted. We'll talk about that later. But for now, let's talk about receiving spiritual information in the first place.

Everyone is Different

People are different from each other—perhaps you have noticed this! But we aren't just different as far as what we look like, and what our voices sound like, and our likes and dislikes. Our ways of perceiving spiritual information are also different. Not everyone perceives spiritual information in the same way.

One helpful thing to understand is called "the clairs." This is not a technical term! But "the clairs" refer to clairvoyance, clairaudience, clairsentience, clairalience, clairgustance, and clairtangency, also known as psychometry.

Coming from a Christian background myself, I know that years ago my alarms went off if I heard the word "clairvoyance." If this is you, I hope you can take a deep breath and just keep reading! It's not as scary as you think.

Each of these "clairs" refers to a specific way of receiving spiritual information. The word "clair" means "clear."

Clairvoyance means clear-seeing, and refers to the ability to intuitively "see" spiritual visions, to access visual-style telepathic information.

Clairaudience means clear-hearing, and refers to the ability to intuitively "hear" spiritual information, as if through the ears, but really through the spiritual ears.

Clairsentience means clear-sensing, and refers to the ability to intuitively sense the emotional sensations of something. This is not necessarily linked to being an "empath."

Claircognizance means clear-knowing, and refers to the ability to just suddenly know something due to the spiritual knowledge just showing up in your brain.

Clairalience means clear-smelling, and it refers to the ability to intuitively smell spiritual information. I know that might sound silly—but an example of this would be smelling your grandma's perfume for "no reason" and just knowing that her spirit is with you.

Clairgustance means clear-tasting, and it's a form of gaining intuitive knowledge through spiritual "taste." An example of this would be feeling like you are tasting a dessert your grandma used to make, and knowing that she is with you.

Clairtangency means clear-touching, and refers to the ability to pick up an object and just sense things about it.

I believe all humans have access to all of "the clairs," but each person naturally comes here having an easier time with some than others. You will have to see for yourself how exactly *you* experience spiritual information. Pay attention to *how* you experience spiritual information flowing into your awareness. It is likely you will be naturally more adept at a few "clairs" than at others, and that is okay.

What About Empaths?

A lot of people love the concept of empaths: people who just sense all the emotions of others around them. And indeed, many people *are* empaths, soaking up other people's toxic emotional garbage everywhere they go.

I personally do not view being an "empath" as any sort of spiritual gift or anything like that. Clairsentience will allow you to *spiritually observe the information* of other people's emotions, but it will *not* make you slurp up those emotions like a sponge. If you are sponging up other people's emotions everywhere you go, to me that is *not* a gift, but a sign of terrible energetic boundaries.

Resolving your boundary issues can solve that problem. I have a class on boundaries in the Free Offerings in allieduzettclasses.com, and a book on boundaries called *30 Days of Belief Work: Boundaries,* and I strongly recommend that you work through both of those so you can overcome the unhealthy tendency to accidentally soak up other people's energetic gunk just by being in the same room!

Beginning to Receive

As you begin to receive more spiritual information, one of my greatest words of advice to you would be to write. Write down everything of significance on your journey. When you feel like you may be receiving a prompting or spiritual information, write it down. If you imagine yourself to be experiencing a divine download, write it down (because maybe you're right!). If you are frustrated, write about that too. Write down the stories of your practice.

Your job in the beginning is nothing more than to pay attention and write things down. Notice what you feel and what information is conveyed by those feelings. Even if the things you feel don't seem to be intuitive—they really are.

If what you are feeling is depression—*that* is your intuition. Depression is your intuition telling you that something is dreadfully wrong. Is it malnutrition and your body suffering from the lack of ingredients to create proper brain chemistry? Is it a terrible living situation or being embroiled in a poisonous relationship? Your intuition knows the real problem, and the way it is communicating with you is your depression.

If what you are feeling is anxiety, *that* is also your intuition. It's your intuition telling you that your top priority needs to be addressing whatever it is that is making you feel so anxious. This could also include shifting your brain chemistry through diet, sleep, hydration, and breath; it could include shifting up your work environment, terminating a terrible relationship, or moving to a new environment. But your anxiety is your intuition.

If what you are feeling is confusion, that, too, is your intuition. That is your intuition telling you that something isn't quite right yet—that something is still missing. Clearing out the stuff standing in between you and clarity can help you find the clarity you seek.

So what feelings are you feeling? Can you trust that the emotions that are showing up for you actually *are* your intuition?

Once you start healing up your big, screaming emotions, *then* you'll be ready to hear the quieter messages that are waiting for you. But if you feel like you're not getting answers, but you *are* filled with big emotions about other things, very often the answer is actually that you can't get better answers until you deal with the big emotions first.

So as you are beginning to take your intuition seriously—just feel. What do you feel? What feelings are showing up for you in your emotions, and where do you feel them in your physical body? Pay attention. Pay attention and write. Writing is how you will make sense of your emotions, validate your emotions, and resolve your emotions. You cannot heal emotions you don't understand, and the way to understand your emotions is to write them down and tell their stories.

This is the first order of business. Feel and write, feel and write, feel and write.

If you don't want to write, well, first, I feel that you are doing yourself a disservice by skipping that part, but even so, feel and pay attention. Intuition is an experience that takes place within your own physical body and within your sacred mind. So it is of utmost importance that you pay attention to what is going on within your physical body and your mind, so you can notice when something changes—when you get a new insight, when you are receiving a message.

Conclusion

In the coming chapters, I have several exercises that will help you practice using your intuition. They will work best in concert with your work from the previous chapters. As you work through these exercises, remember to have patience with yourself and to give yourself a lot of grace. You are practicing and growing in your skill. You have all the time you need to become the master you want to be.

Chapter 12

Asking the Right Questions

It's hard to get good answers when we don't ask good questions. This seems obvious when you read it, but for some reason, this fact seems to escape many people. We can only receive answers as helpful as the questions we ask.

For many years, my prayers were just requests: "Please make sure that this happens. Please fix that. Please do this. Please stop that." When I would go about my day and things would happen, I would think along those lines as well: "I hope *this* happens, I hope *that* doesn't happen." These are not productive thoughts.

How different it is when we go into life asking questions!

Brains are powerful machines, and when we ask questions, our brains search for answers.

When you ask, "Why do bad things always happen to me?" your brain will absolutely generate an answer to that question, and it won't care if the answer is true or not. How much more empowering, then, to start asking, "Why do good things always happen to me?" or "How do so many good things keep flowing into my life?"

Your brain seeks answers to every question you ask. So ask empowering questions.

Some great examples of empowering questions you could start throwing into your daily thoughts would be:

- How do I always find myself at the right place at the right time?
- How come everything in my life goes so well for me?
- How is my body healing so fast?
- How am I receiving so many more intuitive answers than I ever have before?
- Why do good things keep happening to me?
- Why is my life so wonderful?
- Why are my blocks to success melting away before me?
- Why is my life getting easier and happier every single day?
- How is it I always end up with everything I need?
- How does money flow to me today?
- How am I such a good steward of my resources?
- Why do I always have abundance of every good thing?

Asking these sorts of questions as your default mental questions instead of things like, "Why is my life so hard? How come bad things always happen to me?" will seriously change your life.

But this is just the beginning. Because I know you picked up this book wishing that you could get better answers to the questions you are asking of the Divine and of your intuition. You want ANSWERS—but what kind of answers? The kind of answers you receive are directly linked to the kind of questions you are asking.

When people find themselves in a tough situation, they will often start asking, "What should I do?" and I hope you can see that this is a very terrible question.

Why is it a terrible question?

First, it's a terrible question because that same open-endedness is essentially lazy. "What should I do?" is the easiest question in the world to ask because it requires zero effort or thought. It is so open-ended that literally anything could be an appropriate answer.

"What should I do?" Well, you could jump on a trampoline, blow all your savings on a spontaneous trip to Hawaii, go out to dinner with friends, quit your job, buy a new car, invest in Bitcoin.... the sky is the limit when it comes to possible answers to this question. When you ask a question like this, your brain has no boundaries on possible answers, and that makes figuring out what to do extremely difficult. Your brain will still be working to find answers for you, but they will most likely not be productive answers because there are no boundaries on the answers.

To add insult to injury, most people will ask this question of "what should I do" and then not even bother writing about it. When thoughts of importance go unwritten, it's as if they were never thought at all. Even if you ask a bad question, like "what should I do," you *might* get a good answer—but if you don't write that answer down and make a record of it, it can be almost as if you never received the answer at all. Answers are so easy to forget!

Writing down the answers we receive eradicates their ethereal nature and gives them a state of permanence instead. Once the ideas that come into our minds are written down, we can think critically about them in a way that is not possible when they are nothing more than fleeting ephemera.

We must write everything down.

Backing Up For Better Answers

When we don't know what to ask, it's time to back up.

Say you are renting a house and your landlord decides to sell—and you have just one week to get out. There seems to be no other housing option. Your default question is: "What should I do?"

But now you know that this is a terrible question. You know that it is too open-ended and not easily answered through the medium of your body—*and* you realize that it is also the laziest question in the world you could ask.

So you **back up**. In reality, you do want to know what to do––but just asking this is not a good question.

So the *first* question you can have your mind throw into the Universe is: **"What questions should I ask in order to figure out what to do for the best possible housing outcome for my family?"**

If your brain asks that question, you will mostly figure out the questions you need to ask. This is also an open-ended question, but it is the helpful sort of open-ended question that is leading your brain to generate useful answers for you.

Some questions you might be led to ask could include:

- What kind of living situation do I really want?
- What resources could be available to me that I'm not thinking of?
- What miracles might be waiting for me to ask for them?
- What aspects of this situation have I been ignoring?
- Which websites should I look at?
- Who should I talk to about my problem?

- Who should I not talk to about my problem?

Asking questions can be very powerful, but we have to ask the right questions. If we don't know what questions to ask, the answer is simple: **ask what questions to ask**. Set your parameter on what you want from the answers and then get asking. If you don't know what questions to ask to get the right answers, start asking what question to ask.

The Power of Yes-No Questions

Earlier in this book I teach a technique called intuitive calibration, where you learn to use your breath and how your body feels when you inhale and exhale to decipher between a "yes" and a "no."

If the only thing you do differently after learning that technique is shift away from open-ended questions to specific yes-no questions, that will be an enormous win. There is a place for open-ended questions, of course, as we discussed earlier, but adding in plenty of yes-no questions into your inquisitive vocabulary will change everything.

For example, once you have mastered intuitive calibration (in part thanks to lots of deep breaths and nervous system care and hydration and emotional healing), instead of asking "what should I do," you can ask, "Should I post about this on social media?" Then you would breathe and feel if the answer is yes or no, and then take action.

In the case of looking for the new housing situation, you could ask questions like this:

- Should I post about my housing needs on Facebook?

- Should I call a realtor about the problem?

- Would it help if I went for a walk?

Asking yes or no questions and then using intuitive calibration to discern the answers brings immediacy to the answers. You can ask actionable questions and receive instantly actionable answers.

Use open-ended questions to ask your own brain what questions to ask for your ideal outcome, and then use a mix of open-ended questions and yes-no questions to find clarity on whatever is going on in your life.

Taking Action

The other half of asking questions is taking action on the answers. When we ask questions and receive answers *and then don't take action on them*, we lose the "right" to keep getting answers. You may have seen this in yourself. For whatever reason, chronically ignoring the answers we've received seems to lead to a decrease in spiritual sensitivity.

Most of the time, people choose not to act on answers they get because they don't like those answers. The answers seem scary, or too simple, or too illogical. When answers don't make sense, or when they make us uncomfortable, we can be tempted to avoid acting on them.

However, acting on the answers we get, even if they don't make sense, is what strengthens our "muscles" of intuition and intuitive action. Ask for small opportunities to act on intuition, training experiences that won't leave anything in ruins if the experience goes badly. Taking action on the answers we get is absolutely critical to the development of intuition.

Double Checking

Sometimes we get answers that don't feel right. Just to be clear, not every answer that comes into your mind is guaranteed to be correct. Sometimes we do get things wrong.

When you receive an answer and write it down, then you can use intuitive calibration and prayer to revisit the answer and evaluate if it still feels correct or not.

One question I ask in these situations is, "Is this the kind of answer God would give me?" If the answer is yes, that is a good start for me. If the answer is no, then I know I'd probably better do some more digging. Clearing emotions that block clarity can help, and scribbling is a great option for that. Taking some deep breaths, doing some stretches, taking a cold shower, and otherwise resetting yourself can help as well.

Asking a variety of questions can help you find clarity on if you've received the correct answer.

Moving Forward

Sometimes we must move forward even if we are not sure we have the right answer. This is why it is so important to PRACTICE receiving answers in low-stakes environments. More about this in the next chapter.

Moving forward in trust when we don't have all the answers is the definition of intuition. It wouldn't be intuition if you knew for sure it was true! Part of our journey here on the earth is to learn to move forward based on spiritual guidance we hope is true, but don't always know for 100% sure is true.

Conclusion

Asking the right questions and then moving forward with the answers we receive can make a big difference. If you struggle to receive understandable answers, try switching up the types of questions you ask.

Chapter 13

Healing Intuition Trauma

Many of us have trauma around listening to and acting on intuition. This chapter is to help us heal from this trauma.

Scribbling Out Intuition Trauma

I wrote an entire book on what I call "scribbling," a kinesthetic form of energy release. I love scribbling out trauma because you don't have to know anything about it. I fully recommend the entire book, called *The Scribbling Solution* and available on Amazon.

For today, I'm going to give you some prompts to scribble on below.

To use these prompts, keep going until your timer goes off and/or your hand spontaneously makes horizontal 0 shapes, like empty chakras. You can know you are done when even if you TRY to scribble randomly on this issue, your hand naturally reverts back to a gentle, empty horizontal 0 shape. For more explanation and a video demonstration, please see allieduzett.com/scribbling.

1. Imagine the energy of each thing you're going to scribble. What color is it? Gather this energy up into a ball--and then SMASH it with an imaginary hammer until it is no longer a ball, but small pieces.

2. Ask yourself how long it will take to scribble the total energy out. You can muscle test on this or just ask yourself in your mind and see what number pops into your head. Write the time length down.

3. You don't have to scribble it out all at once. If it will take more than 10 minutes to clear, you may want to break it up into smaller chunks and commit to scribbling on it for just 5-10 minutes at a time until the whole thing is clear.

4. Write the prompt down on a fresh sheet of paper and decide how long you will scribble for. You may want to set a timer.

5. Imagine the segment of the negative energy that you will be scribbling out in this moment. Imagine it traveling from the center of your body down through your scribbling arm, into your hand, into your pen.

6. Now scribble and let your hand do the work! You may be surprised at what your hand does and what emotions come up!

Remember, these prompts are designed to work as a set. Please refrain from judging whether or not they "worked" until you have tried ALL of them and scribbled them ALL out. Massive shifts are possible to experience but YOU need to put in the work. Before I give you the scribbling prompts, here is a list of journaling questions to help you self-assess.

Before you get started...

Time to do a quick self-assessment!

Before we begin on the scribbling prompts, let's just take a moment to assess where you are at. Please get out a piece of paper and write to these journal prompts WITH YOUR HAND. Using your physical body for this exercise is important. I recommend writing this down in a place where you will be able to find it again in the future.

1. Why did you seek out this book on intuition and receiving spiritual guidance? What problems have you had with intuition and spiritual guidance in your life?

2. Where in your life are you seeking answers right now?

3. What do you wish you were experiencing with intuition and spiritual guidance that you are not experiencing?

4. Why do you feel you are not having your ideal experience?

5. What emotions come up when you think about the things you wish you were experiencing with your intuition, versus what you are actually experiencing?

6. When you think about next steps with your intuition, what is it inside you that seems to hold you back (if anything)?

7. If you *were* self-sabotaging your own intuition and spiritual guidance, and you knew why you were self-sabotaging, what would your subconscious mind say is the reason?

8. How will you recognize when you are busting through these blocks?

When you have answered all the journaling questions above, it is safe to move on! I do not recommend scribbling without performing this self-assessment first. It is important to pay conscious attention to where you are at the beginning of a process, so it's easier to see your progress along the way.

Working through these journal prompts and these scribbling prompts may take some time—possibly several days or weeks or even months. It's really up to you and the pace you choose. But it WILL be worth your time to do them all!

Scribbling Prompts

Here are the scribbling prompts. Write the words on a sheet of paper and scribble them out.

- Unknown feelings of FEAR OF INTUITION. *After gathering all this energy together and smashing it into tiny pieces, how many minutes will this take to scribble out?* _____

- I fear my own intuition. *After gathering all this energy together and smashing it into tiny pieces, how many minutes will this take to scribble out?* _____

- I fear receiving divine guidance. *After gathering all this energy together and smashing it into tiny pieces, how many minutes will this take to scribble out?* _____

- Intentional confusion as self-sabotage to keep me from doing what I know I need to do. *After gathering all this energy together and smashing it into tiny pieces, how many minutes will this take to scribble out?* _____

- Commitment to self-sabotage with regard to listening to spiritual guidance in my life. *After gathering all this energy together and smashing it into tiny pieces, how many minutes will this take to scribble out?* _____

- Rejection of intuition. *After gathering all this energy together and smashing it into tiny pieces, how many minutes will this take to scribble out?* _____

- Rejection of divine guidance. *After gathering all this energy together and smashing it into tiny pieces, how many minutes will this take to scribble out?* _____

- Not-knowingness of how to perceive spiritual guidance. *After gathering all this energy together and smashing it into tiny pieces, how many minutes will this take to scribble out?* _____

- GUILT over past experiences with intuition. *After gathering all this energy together and smashing it into tiny pieces, how many minutes will this take to scribble out?* _____

- GUILT over past experiences with spiritual guidance. *After gathering all this energy together and smashing it into tiny pieces, how many minutes will this take to scribble out?* _____

- GUILT over things I did in my past that I feel are keeping me from moving forward. *After gathering all this energy together and smashing it into tiny pieces, how many minutes will this take to scribble out?* _____

- Ancestral energies sabotaging my intuitive ability. *After gathering all this energy together and smashing it into tiny pieces, how many minutes will this take to scribble out?* _____

- Ancestral energies sabotaging my ability to hear the voice of the Divine. *After gathering all this energy together and smashing it into tiny pieces, how many minutes will this take to scribble out?* _____

- Failsafes against me removing curses on my intuitive ability (NOTE: it is very important to do this scribble BEFORE doing the next one!). *After gathering all this energy together and smashing it into tiny pieces, how many minutes will this take to scribble out?* _____

- Curses on my intuitive ability and ability to hear the Divine. *After gathering all this energy together and smashing it into tiny pieces, how many minutes will this take to scribble out?* _____

- Generational patterns of intuition struggle. *After gathering all this energy together and smashing it into tiny pieces, how many minutes will this take to scribble out?* _____

- Generational patterns of struggle listening to the Divine. *After gathering all this energy together and smashing it into tiny pieces, how many minutes will this take to scribble out?* _____

- Generational punishments relating to intuition. *After gathering all this energy together and smashing it into tiny pieces, how many minutes will this take to scribble out?* _____

- Personal patterns of struggle with intuition. *After gathering all this energy together and smashing it into tiny pieces, how many minutes will this take to scribble out?* _____

- Not wanting clarity in intuition. *After gathering all this energy together and smashing it into tiny pieces, how many minutes will this take to scribble out?* _____

- Rejecting clarity of intuition. *After gathering all this energy together and smashing it into tiny pieces, how many minutes will this take to scribble out?* _____

- Rejecting clarity of divine messages. *After gathering all this energy together and smashing it into tiny pieces, how many minutes will this take to scribble out?* _____

- External forces passively keeping me from receiving spiritual guidance. *After gathering all this energy together and smashing it into tiny pieces, how many minutes will this take to scribble out?* _____

- External forces intentionally trying to keep me from spiritual guidance. *After gathering all this energy together and smashing it into tiny pieces, how many minutes will this take to scribble out?* _____

- Unsupportive family relating to intuition and spiritual guidance. *After gathering all this energy together and smashing it into tiny pieces, how many minutes will this take to scribble out?* _____

- Unsupportive SELF relating to intuition and spiritual guidance. *After gathering all this energy together and smashing it into tiny pieces, how many minutes will this take to scribble out?* _____

- I don't know how to experience spiritual guidance at all! *After gathering all this energy together and smashing it into tiny pieces, how many minutes will this take to scribble out?* _____

- I am afraid to know how to experience intuition and spiritual guidance. *After gathering all this energy together and smashing it into tiny pieces, how many minutes will this take to scribble out?* _____

- Knowing how to experience spiritual guidance is wrong. *After gathering all this energy together and smashing it into tiny pieces, how many minutes will this take to scribble out?* _____

- It is bad to take action on spiritual guidance. *After gathering all this energy together and smashing it into tiny pieces, how many minutes will this take to scribble out?* _____

- It is bad to receive the answers I am aching to receive. *After gathering all this energy together and smashing it into tiny pieces, how many minutes will this take to scribble out?* _____

- If I receive spiritual answers, I will suffer. *After gathering all this energy together and smashing it into tiny pieces, how many minutes will this take to scribble out?* _____

- People who receive spiritual guidance are crazy. *After gathering all this energy together and smashing it into tiny pieces, how many minutes will this take to scribble out?* _____

- People judge those who receive spiritual guidance and act on it. *After gathering all this energy together and smashing it into tiny pieces, how many minutes will this take to scribble out?* _____

See how you feel after doing all this scribbling! It may take weeks or months to complete it all but I guarantee you will see massive shifts if you do it all.

Healing Pre-Earth Trauma Around Intuition

In my Facebook group, Intuitive Healing with Allie Duzett, one member wrote,

> Is it possible that I "bound" my intuition in this life from a past life? I have this deep fear that if I find it or stir it up or realize I DO have it, that bad things will happen and I will "see" stuff I don't want to see. (think: I see dead people.) I just have this really strong feeling that I am very intuitive but I'm not supposed to be yet...

In my opinion, the answer can absolutely be YES to this question. I write about the role of pre-earth life in current experiences in my book entitled *Deep Past Resolution*, available on Amazon.

I consider myself a Christian and do not personally believe in reincarnation, although I'm cool with it if you believe in it. I do believe, though, that all of us had spirits that existed before we were born, and that we had agency before we were born— and where the ability to make choices exists among imperfect souls, trauma exists, too.

I do believe that many, many people come to Earth already having shut down their intuitive capabilities for one reason or another, often because they were afraid. Historically, people who were very in tune, spiritually speaking, have been maligned, ignored, dismissed, or even burned at the stake. Historically, it has been very dangerous to be a person in tune with intuition. It makes sense that many of us have shut down our intuitive abilities on some level, on purpose. This can be a safety move, even though it also causes its own problems.

If you feel that you are one who bound up your intuition before you were born, or even early on in this mortal life, I have prepared these tapping scripts for you. Tap on your forehead or collarbone and say aloud three times each:

- I honor any pre-earth experiences I may have had that led me to close up my access to my own intuition in this life.

- I honor the intuition-related trauma I have experienced throughout all time.

- It can be safe for me to release my trauma related to acting on my intuition.

- It could be safe to hear spiritual guidance again.

- It could be safe for me to act on spiritual guidance.

- It could be safe for me to act on spiritual guidance, no matter what has happened in my past.

And put your hands on your heart and breathe in.

Guided Imagery: Tube of Light

Imagine a tube of light shining down on your head containing information on intuition: what it is, how to recognize it, how to tell what is your intuition and what is coming from another source. Breathe and imagine this until you get the feeling of a "thumbs up." A sense that the visualization is complete and that on a cellular level, you have now internalized some knowledge about intuition.

Then, imagine a tube of light shining down on your head containing information on divine guidance: what it is, how to recognize it, how to tell what is guidance from the Divine and what is coming from another source. Breathe and imagine this until you get the feeling that the visualization is complete and that on a cellular level, you have now internalized some knowledge about intuition.

Additional Tapping Scripts

These are some additional tapping scripts you can do to help support your intuition. To use them, tap on your forehead or collarbone and say aloud three times each:

- I don't know how I'm healing from any intuition trauma, I only know I am now.

- I don't know how my body and spirit are so easily learning to hear intuition again, I only know they are now.

- I don't know how my body and spirit are so easily learning to discern divine guidance now, I only know that they are.

- It is so easy for me to receive divine answers.

- I easily discern answers to the questions I have.

- I know what questions to ask to get clear answers.

- The right questions to ask flow easily into my mind exactly when I need to ask them.

- I easily discern answers in my physical body.

- When I struggle to get answers I understand, I know what steps to take to heal my physical body so I can understand more easily.

- I deserve to receive answers.

- It can be safe to receive intuitive answers.

- It can be safe to hear divine guidance.

- I give myself permission to receive answers from my intuition and divine guidance.

- When I receive spiritual answers and guidance, I know how to recognize it.

- It is easy for me to take action on the answers I receive.

Go ahead and ask yourself what other tapping scripts you might need. Write them down and get tapping!

It can be easy and so possible to heal from intuition trauma.

Chapter 14

The School of Trust

Early on in my journey, I realized I was going to have to do better at recognizing and acting on the intuitive information I was receiving. I had made a promise that I was going to act on any ideas that came my way, but just committing to that didn't make it easy, and I often wondered if I was doing the right thing.

It came to me that I should ask for training, for little experiences that could teach me big lessons. I started praying that God would send me a tiny prompting during the day, a low-stakes prompting, one that if I acted on would yield benefits but if I didn't, wouldn't ruin my life. I wanted tiny chances to act on my intuition and on spiritual guidance, without risking anything.

The Divine came through for me!

One of my favorite stories involved a cabbage. That fateful Friday morning, I prayed that God would send me a low-stakes opportunity to act on some spiritual guidance. Then I went to Target.

As I was walking around Target, I passed the produce section and a cabbage caught my eye. I felt this unshakeable feeling to buy the cabbage I saw—but I pushed it away, because cabbage is gross and there is no reason why I should buy a cabbage. I went home without any cabbage.

The next day, I got some news. I'll just tell you: I made callbacks for one of my favorite reality TV shows, and I really wanted to be on it! But I knew if I went on it, I would really need laser eye surgery to do my best. My beloved grandma would sponsor laser eye surgery for me, but I would need to get it scheduled ASAP if my eyes would be healed in time for filming. And you can't do laser eye surgery while you are lactating!

At the time I was still nursing my 14-month-old. But I saw that I had limited time to schedule my surgery if I was going to be TV-ready. At the time, it all felt very divinely inspired and I felt like weaning and getting the surgery was the right thing to do. So all in a day, I decided I needed to wean. It wasn't *so* hard; my son was mostly on real food anyway. But what I wasn't prepared for was the PAIN!

It turns out that weaning a child cold-turkey can be extremely painful. By Sunday morning, I was in extreme pain and searching the internet for answers. The answer for weaning pain, of course, is CABBAGE LEAVES.

As soon as I saw that pop up on my screen, I groaned. *Now* I could understand the prompting to buy a cabbage. If I had done that on Friday, I wouldn't be cabbage-less on Sunday. For me, my religious beliefs inspire me to avoid making purchases on Sunday, which I consider my Sabbath, so the fact that I hadn't bought the cabbage earlier meant that now I had to go through a whole day of suffering before I could remedy the situation.

The next day, I rushed out and bought a cabbage right away. I used the leaves throughout the weaning process—and tried a bite of the cabbage that was left over. Imagine my shock when I discovered that I *love* cabbage! I had just never given it a chance. Buying a cabbage helped my body heal in a time of need *and* introduced me to what is now my favorite vegetable.

And since you're wondering, I did *not* end up going on reality TV. Oh well! At the time I was sad but now I don't care. Clearly I have better things to do.

I love this story because to me it is the perfect example of a low-stakes opportunity to practice listening to intuition. I didn't listen to the divine message I received, but it was okay. I suffered a minor inconvenience and took care of it the next day. This is exactly the kind of experience I hope that *you* have as you begin practicing with your intuition.

Setting the Parameters

"Ask and ye shall receive." This a true principle! You can ask for low-stakes opportunities to practice using your intuition and receiving divine messages every day. Who do you ask? Your Higher Power, or if you don't have one, just throw your request into the Universe.

You can start asking now for opportunities every day to experience your own intuition and have low-stakes chances to act on it. As you ask every morning, pay attention to what you feel and sense during the day.

Do you feel a gentle nudge toward the cabbage section in your local Target?

Are your eyes drawn to a particular person, with a little gentle nudge to talk to them?

On the way out of the house, might you have the idea to take something unexpected with you on your trip?

As you pass something on the floor, does a soul-level whisper suggest that you pick it up and put it away?

You can set the parameters of your school of trust. You can ask for help from the Divine to learn to trust your intuition and divine messages in a low-stakes way. But if you do that, you *also* have to act on what you're receiving—even if you think it's just in your imagination. Even if you're not sure if the message was divine or just your imagination.

The secret is that *your imagination is how your intuition speaks to you*. If you feel like you're imagining things... well, you're probably right, and that is great, because it means the process is working.

Practice makes progress. If you feel remarkably un-led in your normal life, ask for practice opportunities and then take action. Pay attention to what happens. You are a scientist and this is your experiment. Catalogue your observations and experiences; write them down and reflect on them. Over time, you will get better at noticing the intuitive suggestions you receive, and you will get better at recognizing how those feelings show up for you.

Just be sure to be specific that you want to learn this skill in low-stakes situations. We want to practice in situations where nothing will go abysmally wrong if we misinterpret something or take the wrong action. We want the worst possible end result to be a laugh and an eyeroll, not a tragedy.

Going Back To School

Did you like school? I didn't. I graduated high school at 16 to start college, and when I got married at 20 with one more semester to go, my dad's big concern was that I would drop out—not because I couldn't handle the work of school, but just because I hated school *so much*. (I did complete my degree.)

So I get it if you super hate school. I hated school every day of my life. *But* if you're going to master listening to divine messages and hearing your own intuition, you've got to go back to school.

As you step into asking every day for learning opportunities, to me, it's critical to view this endeavor as "school." You're going to college to master your own intuitive nature. You're getting your PhD in intuition and connection with the Divine. And so you've got to do the homework. You've got to show up for class. You've got to commit and get the job done.

This is your big chance to "school" yourself through scientific experimentation, testing, observation, reflection. And if you treat these assignments like work, like school, you will find yourself becoming educated on the matter very quickly.

The School of Trust

One question a lot of people have is about trust. How can they be sure they are trusting the right source? If they *do* get an answer, how do they know it's the *right* answer?

You can set the parameters for your experience. Start asking for low-stakes opportunities for yourself to learn when you can and cannot trust the messages you receive.

Or, you could ask for the Divine to install in you a mental alarm that will go off if you are in danger of being misled by false spiritual information, and then you could ask for practice recognizing this alarm in low-stakes situations.

The ability to discern what is a right answer and what is a false answer comes with time and practice. But practice involves taking action. If you are so afraid to do the wrong thing that you don't take action on *anything,* of course it will be very difficult to learn when you actually are getting things right after all. If you set the parameter that you want to learn when to trust and when not to trust in a safe way, and then you start actively seeking these opportunities, I believe you will find them.

Create your school of trust by proactively asking the Divine for daily opportunities to practice. Evaluate your experiences from a lens of patience. Sometimes our opportunities don't make sense at first. For me with the cabbage, at the end of that day, it still didn't make sense why I had been told to buy a cabbage. But a few days later, all had become clear. You may see for yourself how these little daily opportunities play out over time, and this will be the perfect place to practice feeling and acting on intuition and divine guidance.

Involving Other People

One word of caution is warranted. Often people will experience or imagine an intuitive message that involves other people. When this happens, I just want to issue a reminder to always make sure that when your intuitive adventures involve other people, to honor everyone's agency and to act in tact.

I'm thinking of situations where people have felt intuitively led to tell other people shocking information that is unverifiable. For example, in one story, a person felt intuitively led to tell their sibling that the sibling would be married within a year—and then that sibling was *not* married within a year. Or several people have reached out over the years because they felt they had seen omens of death over others and wondered if they should inform them.

My feeling is: when we perceive we have intuited information of this nature that involves other people, it is critical that we do *not* overstep appropriate boundaries. If you have a dream that someone close to you dies, the appropriate thing to do is probably *not* tell that person that they are going to die. If you feel you absolutely must say something, a more appropriate option might be to say that you are thinking about them and had a dream about them recently, and hope they are taking care of their health.

If you feel intuitively led to make someone a promise about the future, always consider the fact that no human can know the future 100% and that agency, human ability to choose, always plays a role. In the earlier example of a person promising their sibling that they would marry within a year, such a promise denies the agency of the people involved.

What if that sibling then decided not to ask anyone out on any dates, and then didn't get married?

My rule is to never issue promises or big speculations. That is unnecessary and counterproductive to your mission of learning in low-stakes scenarios. Every time you issue someone a promise about the future, even if you felt intuitively led to do so, you are creating a level of pressure on yourself and on the entire situation that in my opinion is unnecessary. It can be sufficient to say, "My sense is that something may happen for you this year!" rather than being very specific with timelines and promises.

Carelessness in interpersonal interactions is one primary way people lose trust in their own intuitive abilities. You can be very intuitive, but make a mistake, and if you are forceful about what you feel is true in your conversations with others, and then you are wrong, that can be absolutely devastating emotionally. It is better to use wisdom in interacting with people and to be judicious in how you verbally present your intuitive thoughts and experiences. It is not your job to convince anyone of anything.

Asking For the Unmistakable and Obvious

One thing I like to do in my prayers is ask for my answers to be unmistakeable and obvious. I ask the Divine to ensure that there is *no possible way* that I misinterpret what is told to me. I strongly recommend setting this intention.

Here are some tapping scripts to help prime your mind to accept unmistakeable and obvious answers. Tap on your forehead and/or collarbone and say aloud three times each:

- Even though I have struggled to feel intuitively led in the past, I now find that unmistakeable and obvious spiritual guidance flows to me every day.

- It is easy for me to feel intuitively led because the messages from my intuition and the Divine are unmistakeable and obvious.

- It could be safe to accept divine messages that are unmistakeable and obvious.

- I can trust myself to act on divine messages that are unmistakeable and obvious.

Conclusion

Learning how to trust your intuition and divine guidance comes with time and practice. The best way to get this practice in is to ask for it. Ask specifically for low-stakes opportunities to practice with, and then act on the things you think might be intuition, even if you are not sure. Be wise in how you take action, especially when other people are involved, and be sure to ask that your messages are unmistakeable and obvious. You set the parameters on your experience.

Of course, remember that before you do this, you should have attended to your physical body and the alignment situations mentioned in the previous chapters.

Chapter 15

The Power of Writing For Powerful Insight

Writing can be an incredible way to receive divine guidance and illumination from your own intuition. Some people call this "prayer journaling" (in fact, that is often how I refer to this concept!), but you could also call it "inspired writing."

Writing things down is one of the most powerful things we do as humans. Writing makes things permanent, adds power. When we write something down, it stops being a mere thought and becomes a true *thing*, an object, a written word on a physical medium.

Writing takes transient, ephemeral, fleeting thought and makes it into something that can be reviewed, studied, pondered, considered again and again.

Normally when we think, our thoughts go into our brain and out again pretty fast. Have you ever had a big insight and thought: oh wow! I'm a genius! But a few hours later, you couldn't even remember what your thought was?

When we put things into writing, we grant them immortality—or at least, a much longer version of mortality.

When we try to receive spiritual guidance with just our minds and don't even bother to try writing anything down, we make a grave mistake. Being willing to write down our inspirations opens the way to receive more. When we write down the spiritual guidance that comes to us, it gives us an added ability to act on the information. I believe the Divine honors our attempts to take guidance seriously when we write things down, and I believe that the act of writing things down opens up the way to receive more information.

So how do we write things down for spiritual guidance? What does that even mean?

Journaling for Spiritual Insight

I have kept a journal since I was 14 years old, and I'm eternally grateful that I have. Probably everyone has crazy teenage years, and I was no different—but journaling kept me sane. I would write every day, and just pour all my crazy emotions onto the pages. And because I had a safe place to vent all my feelings, I feel like I escaped those years much more emotionally stable than many of the other teenagers I knew then and know now.

So I am strongly in favor of everyone having a journal, including you. I journal about my emotions and about things that happen in my life that I don't want to forget.

But prayer journaling, journaling for spiritual insight, is a little different.

In the introduction of this book, I wrote about the different

sources of spiritual guidance: guidance originating from our Source, the Divine; guidance originating from our own Higher Self, also known as intuition; and guidance originating from our physical bodies. When it comes to journaling for guidance, the first step to take is to choose which of these three you want to be hearing from. And I think all three are worth talking to!

You start by drafting a letter to God or your Higher Power; your own intuition; or to your physical body. Write a letter and fully pour out your feelings and thoughts, and ask the questions you want to ask. When you're done, skip a line and write a letter back to yourself just as you imagine it in your mind.

As you write, don't judge what comes to you. Just allow it to flow until it feels done. I recommend against reading it as you go. Just write and write and write until it's done, and *then* go back and reread it—and I recommend praying over it as well, and using your logical mind to see if the answer you got made sense. I believe God speaks to us in our mind AND in our heart, and so to me when I do this I always like to double check if I feel this is the kind of answer God (or my Higher Self, or my body) would give me.

If you don't know what questions to ask in your prayer journaling, you can also just ask that question: "What should I ask?" You are allowed to ask whatever you want and see what comes to you. Just write down whatever flows into your mind, and then go back afterwards and make sure what you received feels right to your mind and your heart.

Troubleshooting Journaling For Spiritual Guidance

This is a simple exercise to explain, but some people really struggle with it for a few reasons.

First, they can feel like they are making up the answers they get, and then they struggle to trust what they receive because they feel like they made it up. I feel like this is an understandable worry if you are trying to write down a message from the Divine, but a very silly worry if you are trying to get a message from your intuition or your physical body. Since your intuition and your physical body *literally ARE YOU*, of COURSE when you get a message from them, it will feel like you are making it up. You *are!* That is exactly why the message is so accurate and powerful. "Making it up yourself" is where the power is!

This can feel counterintuitive, so I recommend just trying it a few times and reserving your judgment. Just try it, and observe what happens over a few days.

Early on in my journey with this, I had a situation where I was dealing with a very difficult client. This client was a survivor of horrific, severe and extreme child abuse and while I call her a "client," I actually worked on her for free, and on top of that, her case was so extreme she actually moved in with me because she needed constant supervision. Ah! It was a tough time, even though it was very rewarding and she experienced some massive healing.

When she finally moved out, the first thing I did after dropping her back off at her apartment was this: prayer journaling. My question was brief: "God, what message do you have for me about this person I've been helping?"

I skipped a line and got writing, just transcribing whatever words came into my head, and what came to me was two separate paragraphs. They didn't relate to each other at all. I read them and thought: *this makes no sense.* So I put my journal down and got to work doing other things.

But just an hour or two after this, my client called me up in distress. She had an urgent question—and as she asked it, I was floored to realize that the answer was the first paragraph I'd written down as part of my prayer journaling that morning.

"Wow, okay," she said, "Thank you. That makes me feel better. But—what about this other unrelated thing?"

And I couldn't believe it: her second question was the topic of that second unrelated paragraph I'd received earlier that morning. I read her the paragraph aloud, and that was that. Her questions were answered and she was able to peacefully make the transition back to living in her own home.

I tell this story because I love how I received information in my prayer journaling that made no sense at the time, but just a few hours later, it all came together. Very often, this occurs. So I hope as you start trying this, you don't judge what comes or give up on it too soon. Just write, and if things don't make sense right away, come back to them later—later that day, or perhaps later that week, month, or year. Over time, you may find that what you receive makes a lot more sense than you initially thought it did.

Another reason people can struggle with this is when they feel "blocked" and like they literally cannot "hear" or perceive any kind of words to even write down.

When that happens, of course the first priority needs to be everything else we've talked about in this book so far: breathing and breathwork, and physical body nervous system care. But the next thing to be done is emotional work, because very often when blocks like this occur, if it isn't a nervous system problem or the result of chronic shallow breathing, it's most likely an emotional problem.

The number one thing I recommend to start with for clearing emotional blocks to revelation is called scribbling, and I write about it at length in the book *The Scribbling Solution*, available on Amazon. I highly recommend that book if you're interested in learning how to scribble for weight loss, healing health conditions, and other applications.

I'll teach you the basics of scribbling momentarily, but before I do, I know that some people really struggle to see results with scribbling. So before I teach you the basics, I want to address *that*. Go ahead and take out your fingers, and tap on your forehead or collarbone and say aloud three times each:

- I am now accepting the divine instructions on how to scribble effectively, straight to my energy field.

- My body, spirit, and energy now understand how to use kinesthetic transmutation of energy to clear emotional blocks easily and gently.

- I don't know how my body, spirit, and energy all know how to use scribbling so easily to clear my emotional blocks permanently, I only know they know it now.

- Scribbling effectively is so easy for me now.

- My hand naturally makes that horizontal 0 shape on its own and when it does, I instantly feel the release. It feels amazing.

- My body loves clearing emotional blocks through scribbling.

Okay! Breathe that in, and this is how to scribble for emotional clearing.

Scribbling for Emotional Clearing

For those that prefer video instruction, I have a video explanation of how to do this form of emotional release at allieduzett.com/scribbling.

To do this exercise, all you need is paper and a pen. Actually, you don't even need a pen: the last time I did this exercise, it was with my finger on the screen of my phone. I have also simply used my hand in the air. A blunt crayon and a scrap paper work as well. Once you understand the concept, you can make this exercise work for you in many different contexts.

It is so easy.

The first step is to **identify what it is you're trying to work out**. To release blocks to receiving spiritual guidance, you can just write down, "The block to receiving spiritual guidance about X issue." You don't have to know what the block is, just that you have one.

Label the top of your paper with whatever it is you're working on, as vaguely or as specifically as you can or want to. If you know you are having trouble receiving revelation because you are afraid of the answer you might get, you could label your paper "my fear of receiving an answer I don't want to hear." If you think you might be having trouble receiving guidance because you honestly believe you are incapable of receiving guidance, you could label your paper "I don't believe I am capable of receiving spiritual guidance." And so on.

However you feel you should label your paper, label your paper—as vaguely or specifically as you need to.

Step two is to imagine all the energy of the negative thing you're trying to clear as a specific color. I usually see mine as dark gray. Imagine all of that color gathering together throughout your body, and queuing up in the hand you'll be using.

And then:

SCRIBBLE!!!

Let your conscious mind take a break: it's not invited to this party. This is your subconscious mind's time to take over. Imagine the color of the negativity you're releasing going through your hand, into the writing utensil, and then out onto the paper (or even the screen of your phone, if you're scribbling with your finger on the screen).

If you're having trouble just letting your hand do its thing, then switch hands and let your non-dominant hand do the drawing.

The point is to let your body feel and release the emotion in a safe (but possibly intense!) way.

You may be surprised at how your hand and even your arm seems to take on a life of its own. That's what always shocks me, even though I know it will happen. I've done this exercise countless times, but it's still always such a surprise.

Keep going until your hand *spontaneously* makes **one single horizontal 0 shape,** a zero on its side, over and over again, right on top of itself. When you try to force your hand to scribble, it should naturally come back to making the empty hole shape. It is a shape symbolic of *emptiness.* If your ending horizontal 0 shape ends up filled in, or creating many loops that fill each other in, you are not done. You know you are done when no matter how you try to scribble on that issue, your hand naturally comes back to the empty horizontal oval.

Here's an experience that I had with this exercise once: I could feel a weird turbulence in my emotions and I didn't know what it was. So I grabbed a scrap paper and a blunt crayon, and told my hand to have at it. At first I scribbled back and forth to the left, but then it got crazier and crazier until it was a dark blob on the lower right side of the scribble mass. The scribble ended with figure-8-type loops underneath that.

Next, I felt like asking myself, "Is there an energy that I need to heal this issue?" I didn't know what they meant, but I wrote down some numbers that felt right. These numbers just came into my mind and I don't know what or what they meant, but I did feel better once I'd written them down. I'm sure they had a meaning but I know that you don't need to understand everything that comes into your mind to help heal a situation. You can ask yourself what "energies" you need to heal the emotional turbulence you are working to clear, and just write down whatever comes to you: numbers, names, flowers, ideas, whatever. Draw, color, write whatever comes to mind as something that will heal the issue.

You will find as you experiment with this technique that many things can happen--and you can feel very different afterwards. Even if what comes up during the exercise doesn't make sense.

Going back to my example, at that point, I felt like I could finally ask what the emotion was. The sense I felt in my heart was "self-resentment." I asked what I was resenting about myself, and got no answer. Later, I realized it was because I no longer had that self-resentment--it had been all scribbled out!

Once again, when your scribble is done, **you will know it because your hand will spontaneously create horizontal 0 shapes.** This has been true for virtually all of my clients, regardless of their background or whether I told them about this ahead of time. So **keep scribbling until your hand spontaneously creates horizontal 0s.** You will know you are truly done when you actively try to scribble and your hand naturally goes back to making that 0 shape instead.

To me, that horizontal 0 shape is symbolic of emptiness: it's a void where that trauma was. I love getting to that point in this exercise because when my hand starts making that shape, and I try scribbling a different way and just go back to that shape, I feel so different and so much happier.

For extra goodness, you can imagine filling up that empty 0 shape with light, symbolic of your own healing and choice to fill spaces with light that used to be full of trauma.

You will most likely want to throw away the paper when you are done, also. Typically, my used scribble papers have a very dark feeling to them. Often, it is worth it to me to pinch them by their corner and walk outside to throw them in the outside trash, and then come in and wash my hands.

I wrote earlier that you can actually do this exercise on your phone. One of my students discovered this when she tried it out on a scribbling app she'd gotten for one of her kids. If you do this exercise using your phone, afterwards, you will want to imagine light from the Divine coming down from the heavens and washing any residual darkness out of your phone!

When it comes to clearing blocks to receiving spiritual guidance, this exercise is fabulous because it takes something that can seem huge and intense, and allows us to eradicate it without muscle testing, without fancy magnets, without really anything. You don't need to be properly polarized or grounded to clear trauma this way--you don't even need to be sure what the trauma is. You just choose what you want to work on and get started.

One precaution with this exercise is to possibly be mindful of the magnitude of what you seek to use it for. **Very large traumas may be too much to try scribbling out all at once.** And once you start scribbling, you don't want to stop until you've gotten that horizontal 0 shape.

So it can be wise to *set the intention ahead of time that the trauma you wish to work on will be separated into smaller pieces that can be scribbled out in five-minute increments.* **I like to imagine the trauma I am working with, and then imagine smashing it with a hammer into smaller pieces that are more manageable to scribble out.**

This exercise sounds very easy when you read about it, but after a few minutes your arm can really get tired! So it's good to break down the trauma you want to clear into smaller pieces before you commit to scribbling it out all the way.

A story comes to mind of one client in particular who was a victim of extreme abuse as a child. When she attempted to scribble on it, she did not break down the traumas into smaller pieces first and ended up scribbling for many, many minutes, completely destroying many sheets of paper--scribbling right through the papers--and still did not find resolution.

When you are working with a trauma that is large, often you want to break it down first by imagining it breaking into smaller pieces, and then work on it one piece at a time until it is resolved.

It's like eating an elephant. How do you eat an elephant? One bite at a time.

How do you resolve and release all the traumas, blocks, and resistances holding you back? One five-minute increment of work at a time. Over time, those five-minute investments in your health and wellness will really pay off. It's the law of compound interest!

If you get started scribbling not realizing how big of an energy something is, you can at that time mentally chop off that energy into a smaller piece and set the intention that you will finish scribbling out this portion of energy now. That is an easy way to fix things if you accidentally "bite off more than you can chew" with this work.

Analyzing Your Scribbles

One question I get fairly regularly about this exercise is if the shapes you scribble mean anything. My opinion is that they must, but I have no idea what the shapes mean, and it feels **extremely unimportant** to me to analyze them.

To me, the important thing here is using the technique to release and resolve trauma without needing to dig into lots of pesky details.

The beauty of scribbling as a release technique is **how much you DON'T need to know**. The point of scribbling is to release negative energies *without* the hassle of grounding, polarizing, muscle testing, and anything else.

To me, analyzing scribbles after the fact just adds an unnecessary complication to the work. So, I say: don't bother with that, it's a waste of time. You could use those five minutes you're analyzing your scribble to just scribble something else out! To me personally, that is a better use of time.

If you feel inspired to psychoanalyze your scribbles, that is fine with me--just know that I will be unlikely to offer additional wisdom about their meaning. To me, the only meaning of a scribble that matters is: what was once in, is now OUT!

HOORAY!

For more on how to use scribbling for anxiety, depression, weight loss, relationships, and manifestation, please order the book *The Scribbling Solution* on Amazon.com.

Prayer Journaling Challenge

My challenge to you is to try journaling for spiritual guidance **every day for 14 days**. That is just two short weeks! But you will see for yourself how as you practice this every day for two consecutive weeks, that you will set in motion more healing and more insight than you have received regularly ever before.

At first, things might be hard or feel like they don't "flow." Some people might get frustrated or want to give up. That's okay—but I do hope you'll keep going. Practice makes progress. What you might consider is to set a timer and commit to work on this exercise for anywhere from 5-30 minutes a day for that two-week period. If you don't seem to get anything to write down, that's fine. Just try for the 5-30 minutes, however many minutes you choose, and when the timer is up, go do something else and know that you gave it a real solid try. Then try again tomorrow.

I am confident that you will see some growth in your ability to receive spiritual information during this two-week challenge. When you see that growth too, I invite you to come share it in my Facebook group, Intuitive Healing With Allie Duzett! We will love to hear your experience!

Tapping Scripts for Successful Prayer Journaling

Here are some tapping scripts to support you in your prayer journaling. Tap on your forehead or collarbone and say aloud three times each:

- I don't know how I so easily receive spiritual information when I journal, I only know that words flow easily to me.

- I choose to be open to spiritual guidance that I receive in writing.

- I can easily hear and feel spiritual insights that I easily put down in writing.

- I don't know how my spirit and body are so easily releasing any blocks I've had to receiving written revelation, I only know that those blocks are clearing now.

- Every day, receiving spiritual information comes more and more easily to me, and I am fulfilled.

- I look forward to my prayer journaling time every day.

You may want to do these tapping scripts daily for at least two weeks.

Ideas for Prayer Journaling Topics

I'm assuming most people reading this book are reading it because they have specific concerns they want to receive inspiration about. If you already know what you need more information on, then write about that and see what you get! But if you need some ideas for prayer journaling, here are some examples of questions you could ask, just to get your mind going:

- Body, why am I experiencing _____ pain?

- Body, what specific action could I take today to support my nervous system health?

- Body, are there any foods you would prefer I stop eating?

- Body, are there any foods you wish I would start eating?

- Body, talk to me about exercise. What do you wish I knew about exercise at this time?

- Self, what are the lessons I need to be learning from the particular experience that I'm going through right now?

- Self, what unresolved emotions are your top priority for me to address this week?

- Self, if you could tell me one thing that would help me today, what would it be?

- Self, what within me is causing strife and trouble in my relationships with others? What is your advice on how to change and heal from that?

- Self, what is the number one thing I need to eradicate from my life right now so I can live in greater alignment with my higher purpose?

- Self, what thoughts do you have for me on my journey to discover my soul purpose at this time?

- Divine Source, what message do You have for me today?

- Divine Source, what unresolved stuff from my past is holding me back now?

- Divine Source, what is Your perspective on the particular situation I'm going through right now?

- Divine Source, I'm worried about _____. What insights do You have for me on this?

- Divine Source, how can I feel Your love today?

These were just a few examples of the sorts of things you could write. Please use them as inspiration for your own journaling!

Conclusion

Journaling for spiritual insight can be an incredibly simple way to receive powerful spiritual guidance. If you run into trouble, there are many things you can do to troubleshoot—but one of the best things you can do is commit to trying this technique for two weeks in a row. I am so excited for the insight you will receive this way. Remember if you have an incredible experience with this to please mention it in your review of this book on Amazon!

Chapter 16

A Life-Changing Self-Healing Exercise

Journaling for spiritual insight can be very powerful, but sometimes you need something a little different. When that happens to me, I try the exercise I'm about to teach to you.

This is one of my favorite, most powerful self-healing exercises. I try to do it as often as I can, which unfortunately isn't very often, but when I do it, it is POWERFUL. Seriously, all-caps powerful. I always feel an incredible shift with this exercise.

I designed this exercise for the purpose of emotional healing, but the secret with this exercise is that very often, when people try it, they end up learning information they were looking for. When you go into this exercise with the problem you are seeking answers to, very often you can discover the answer.

You need a pen and paper for it, but it's not a journaling exercise. Those are just for taking notes because I can guarantee you will experience things you will want to write down from this journey.

It's a multi-step process, and these are the steps:

STEP 1: Prepare. If there's an issue that's bothering you, prepare by identifying it clearly. What is the problem at hand? A physical problem like infertility, a bone that won't heal, back pain, or cancer? An emotional problem like inexplicable rage, a lethargic depression pulling you down, or a fear of interacting with other people? A spiritual problem like a lack of desire to pray, a feeling of distraction keeping you from meeting your spiritual potential, or an anger with God or spirituality generally?

Identify the problem clearly. In this exercise, we go to the root.

STEP 2: Find a quiet place, get comfortable, and get ready to FEEL! For real, be sure you're in a place where you will not be disturbed. I like to set a timer for one hour and set the intention that the exercise will be complete within that hour time.

STEP 3: If you are a praying person, tell God your problem and why you are seeking to understand the root of the issue. If you are not a praying person, just verbalize these ideas to the Universe generally. In your mind, state: "I'm willing and ready to feel the things I haven't wanted to feel that are at the root of this problem. Please, bring them to my attention! I'm ready to feel!!"

STEP 4: Feel the feels.

Seriously, this is an emotional thing. I like to take notes during Step 4. I like to write out my issues during Step 1, rewrite them in the form of a letter to God(/the Universe) in Step 3, and then during Step 4, I let the tears roll… and when I can figure out why I am feeling what I'm feeling, I write it down.

You may be very surprised at what comes up. You might feel a shaking anger with someone or a situation you don't even remember. Maybe you'll feel a sudden panic, or a dread or fear. Maybe it's an uncontrollable rage or a sinking depression.

The important thing is to feel it and not quit until it's done. You have. To feel. It all. The way. *You have to feel it all the way.* **You have to feel it all the way**.

You might cry, you might shake, you might have an incredible urge to scream. Just scream. I scream into a pillow because of course the only time I ever have free to do this, my kids are asleep and I don't want to wake them up! Pound the floor with your fists, do whatever it takes to get the feelings out. Just feel. Sob and sob and sob. Know in your soul that these feelings will not break you. Getting them out of your system is vital to your physical and emotional health and wellbeing.

When the feeling part is done, you will know it. I usually budget a full hour to 90 minutes for just feeling from this exercise. But when it's done, I get this "done" feeling.

You might feel like writing something down that commemorates the "doneness:" "Good job! This is done!" on your sheet of paper. It won't feel COMPLETE, which is to say, you will still feel transitional, and the rest of the day you might feel "off" or just like you're processing some emotions. But you'll be able to handle your emotions and get through the rest of the day. After a good night's sleep, you will feel very different.

Step 5: Recover. It usually takes a full day to recover from this exercise. Drink lots of water, rest, and notice what is different. Notice how you feel a stillness where there used to be turbulence. Isn't that beautiful?

Using This Technique For Receiving Answers

When you are using this self-healing technique for receiving spiritual answers, the process may transcend mere emotional healing. You might set aside the hour in a quiet place and identify the problem: "I can't receive spiritual guidance on X issue." Then tell the Divine that you are ready to feel the feelings that are blocking you from receiving the guidance you need. Feel the feelings thoroughly, and just know that when the hour is up, the feelings will be cleared. Write down whatever information comes into your mind, even if it doesn't make sense. Then, in the aftermath, rest and recover. See for yourself how in coming days things seem clearer and easier.

Opening to Healing When You Struggle to Be Open

This exercise is one of my favorites, but I know that sometimes it can be hard to do when you aren't used to being open to spiritual information. The power here, though, comes from putting in the effort and making the commitment to do the work.

Setting aside a specific time, going to a quiet place, and committing to sit there and feel things has a lot of power in it. The first time I tried this, I wasn't sure if it would work, but I set aside the hour anyway and told myself and God that I was not going anywhere until the hour was done. It took some time to get the feelings going, and I want to talk about that quickly.

I've done this exercise numerous times now, but still it can take me some time to get the emotional ball rolling. It can feel kind of like my brain is stretching out its hands and just groping around in the darkness for some feeling to latch onto.

So I might go into this hour feeling basically normal but a little annoyed about the problem I want to resolve, and then once I close the door in my quiet place, I set my intentions and just start breathing. I think about my problem and just allow any feelings to show up. And sometimes they don't show up at first. Sometimes I've had a situation where I hear a word like "anger," but I don't feel angry yet. When that happens, I'll mentally search out any anger and practice emoting anger—I mean like I'll literally punch the floor or make angry sounds.

Emoting the feeling, or in other words, expressing the feeling with my physical body, can get things moving, even if I don't emotionally feel the feeling at first.

My purpose in telling you this is to encourage you. Trying this exercise may feel silly at first and you may not immediately connect to any emotions. Again, you might feel like any emotions that come up are things you're just making up. If you feel like you're making it up, that is actually even better. Because it is YOU. And you SHOULD be making it up. Whatever you need to express has originated with you, and therefore was made up by you. So if you feel like you are making up an issue, that is exactly right and exactly as it should be. It is no reason for alarm or distress; just sink into it and breathe on through it.

And always remember to put that time boundary on the event. This exercise will dislodge a lot of emotional stuff and you will most likely feel different in your body for up to 24 hours after performing this exercise. So you don't want to leave the option open for the exercise to last for a very long time. I feel an hour is the perfect length of time: just long enough to get the emotional ball rolling and expressed, but still short enough that it's not completely overwhelming and horrible.

When the Self-Healing Exercise Is Really Intense

The fact is that this exercise can be intense... really intense. To be honest, when I do it with pure intention, it can seriously feel like the intensity of the emotions that flow up could rip apart my very soul. I can remember three separate times I've done this exercise where I felt such emotional pain, it seriously felt like it was ripping my spirit apart and like I was emotionally going to die. Have you ever felt like that? It was a crazy experience to me, and the first time I really felt like I understood what it feels like to have so much emotional pain that it's almost physically painful to experience it within the vessel of the body.

So this exercise can be extremely intense and I just want to mention that. This is one reason it is so important to have a time boundary on it: clearly choosing that the experience will be complete within a single hour has been the one thing that has made this exercise bearable to me. When I open myself up to fully feeling the emotional pain I've been trying to fight, it hurts like the dickens, for real. *But* knowing that it will only go on for a single hour makes it bearable. I can scream, cry, kick the floor, pull my own hair, and generally feel extremely horrible—but I know that within 60 minutes, the feelings will be gone, and in the aftermath there will just be emptiness and peace.

When we struggle to receive spiritual guidance, many times it can be because our own body or spirit is blocking the information, for one reason or another. Often we block it because of subconscious programming or just an overload of internal emotional pain that makes it impossible to hear the still, small voice of spiritual guidance very clearly. This exercise is an intense but time-bounded way to quickly pass through emotional pain that is keeping it hard to hear divine guidance and our own intuition.

The trick when it gets very intense is to remember that it's just for an hour. When it's done, you'll feel pretty tired, but you shouldn't feel terrible. You should feel almost like you've given birth, like your body has expelled something big and difficult to release, but once it's out, it's time to rest and get used to life without that energy in your space.

Conclusion

Doing this exercise as necessary can help you clear out space in your own heart, so you can more easily hear revelation and spiritual guidance. Be sure to drink enough water, get enough rest, and keep breathing through. You may see some enormous shifts in your life as you use this technique.

Chapter 17

When There Is No Answer

When I sat down to write this book, a good friend of mine said to be sure to talk about "when there is no answer." When you pour out your soul to the heavens for guidance and comfort and receive... a whole bunch of nothing.

I believe that if you go through this entire book and do all of the exercises inside, eventually, most likely you will *not* have many experiences in the future where you receive no spiritual guidance whatsoever. But occasionally we know that will be the case. Even Jesus, during the Atonement in Gethsemane, was left alone. Remember the famous words: "My God, my God, why hast Thou forsaken Me?" Even Jesus had massive trials where God's presence felt absent. All of us can, from time to time, expect to experience the same.

I believe that this experience is one that ought to be far and few between. This should not be the norm for humankind. In normal life, divine guidance and spiritual answers should be very easy to come by, IF we are in alignment and taking good care of our bodies and spirits. But even when we are doing everything right, there is still the potential for us to receive no answer, and to feel forsaken. The following are perspectives to consider when this situation is the case for you: when even after you have done every single thing in this book, you still sense no guidance.

Stop Me If It's Wrong

When I was in college, I decided that I wanted to change my major from English to Environmental Science. I'd fallen in love with the field after an introductory class on the topic, and I just felt this huge craving to devote my brain to science (while I was still alive!). I would pray and pray and ask if this was the right choice, and get no answer. But I just wanted to make this change so badly.

Finally, I decided I was just going to do it, since God apparently had nothing to say about it. I went up to the office for the College of Life Sciences and I waited to hear an answer. I heard nothing. I said in my heart, "God, just stop me if it's wrong!" And I changed my major. He didn't stop me.

But immediately after I signed my name on the dotted line and handed over the paperwork, I heard that voice in my mind: "This is the last time you can change your major. This was a fine choice, but you can't change your major anymore."

Very well!

Sometimes we pray and pray and search and search and find no answers. In those times, when action is required, my default setting is to do what I did when I changed my major. I decide what I want to do, make sure I truly feel no warnings about it either way, and then tell God to stop me if it's wrong. I invite you to consider practicing with the same technique.

Think About It Tomorrow

Sometimes the things we need answers for are not related to actions we need to take or decisions we need to make, but rather spiritual concepts we need to make sense of. What do we do when serious concerns about religion or other aspects of our faith journeys crop up—and we pray and feel no clear answer?

As I was thinking about this section, I thought of Scarlett O'Hara in Gone with the Wind, and her famous motto: "I'll think about that tomorrow." Scarlett uses this motto in a possibly irresponsible way, using it to defer seriously considering her own moral flaws and failures. But the concept here, of deferring worry, I actually appreciate.

When it comes to big questions, the big potentially faith-shaking things, if you don't get an answer, you can come to your own conclusion and ask God to make it clear to you if you are wrong, or alternatively, you can choose to hold space for the reality that you don't understand everything, and that maybe now is not the time to know everything.

For me, I have long ago come to find peace in the idea that I don't know everything and that it's really not the time for me to know everything.

There are many big questions about the universe that I just don't see the point in worrying about right this exact minute.

I tell God that I'd like an answer, but I understand if that's not the best thing for me right now, and in that case, I guess I'll think about that tomorrow.

I do believe that God is a way smarter guy than I am, and that sometimes things that are true are things that are not very fun or very culturally appropriate in our modern culture. It actually is safe to put an intentional pause on your worrying and questioning and just trust that things will make sense over time.

Drawing From An Empty Well

Sometimes we want answers to our questions to come instantly, easily, without hesitation—and without additional work on our end. This is the place where I remind us all that it's very difficult to draw from an empty well.

If you are praying and praying about where to move to, and getting no answers, maybe it's time to read some articles on the towns you're thinking about, or go visit them in person.

If you're trying to decide what to do about your employment situation, maybe it's time to research the options you are looking at more thoroughly, book some meetings with friends in the field, and visit possible places of employment just to see how you feel there.

When we don't know what to do, sometimes the call is to consciously seek additional information. Read a book on the topic, go somewhere related, visit with someone who knows more about what you need to know about.

Very often, as we seek more information about our question, we come to helpful answers. If you get stuck not knowing what to think or what to do, I invite you to consider seeking more information in any way you can.

Praying for a Stepping Stone

If you have a big decision ahead of you about something you need to do or some mental conclusion you need to make, and you feel no answers, sometimes it can be helpful to shift the focus. I wrote about this in the chapter on asking questions, but this is another take on the concept.

When we are getting no answers to something big, sometimes it can be helpful to ask new questions that are smaller, intermediary questions.

Maybe instead of praying to find a new house, you could pray to meet someone who will help you find your perfect house.

Maybe instead of asking if going to this particular college is the right choice, you could ask about a specific class, or about working with a specific professor.

You can use your powerful brain to evaluate the answers you are seeking, and look for adjacent questions or sideways answers to look for also. Sometimes we will struggle getting answers to certain things, but find our answers in a more roundabout way when we look at the situation from other angles and ask new questions.

Rest in Peace

I believe so strongly in the principle of trust in the Divine. When we are not getting answers on timetables we seek, or in ways we feel clear about, I feel so strongly that we can still find peace. We are allowed to rest in peace–while we are still alive! We can find rest and we can find peace even when we don't have all the answers.

Here are some tapping scripts to help us find peace even when we're not getting answers as quickly as we wish we were. To use them, tap on your collarbone and say the words aloud at least three times each. You can use these tapping scripts whenever you need a boost of peace about seemingly unanswered prayers.

1. It can be safe to feel peace even if I am feeling ignored.

2. It can be safe to feel peace even when I don't have all the answers.

3. I can rest and find peace even though I don't know everything.

4. It can be safe to rest where I am, even if I feel pressure to make a decision.

5. Even though I don't know how I feel so much peace right now, I only know I feel more and more peace with every calming breath.

6. I choose into rest and peace as I consider the decisions before me.

7. I am open to feeling peace even when I don't have all the answers.

8. I can trust that all answers will flow to me in their perfect timing.

9. I accept that answers flow to me in perfect timing— even when it is timing that is slower than I wish it was!

10. I choose peace over stress when I don't have all the answers.

Put your hands on your heart and breathe in! It really and truly can be safe to find peace even when you don't have all the answers. Everything happens in perfect timing—including when we all receive our answers.

Conclusion

Sometimes we don't get all the answers on the timetables we would choose. This is okay and even good. Everything really does happen in the divine timing. We have the tools we need to research, make decisions, and take action even if we don't always feel 100% divinely led in every single decision.

Chapter 18

A Final Note

My friend, just look at us! I wrote this whole book and you just read it. I am so proud of both of us!

Learning to know and trust your own ability to receive spiritual answers is no small task, as you have learned. There's a lot to do to prepare your body and soul to be a living machine for gathering answers. This book is chock full of practical suggestions of things you can choose to do in your daily life to make your intuitive abilities that much stronger. The next step, of course, is to actually take action. Implement the things you've learned, even if it's just in small ways. Taking just a little bit of action over time will yield bigger results than you can imagine.

And I believe in you.

If this book was helpful to you, there are some additional things you can do. Of course, first, would you please **leave a review of this book on Amazon?** Reviews are how people decide if they're going to bother reading a book or not. If you feel this information could be valuable to other humans on the planet, it would be a great service--greater than you realize—to take the time to leave a review.

Second, I invite you to get all signed up with the Free Offerings in allieduzettclasses.com, and to join my Facebook group, Intuitive Healing with Allie Duzett. It is a great group and you will love being a part of it. The people in that group are my favorite people of all.

Of course, come find me on Youtube; just look up my name to find my channel. And if this work was helpful to you, please tell a friend about it. This is how we will change the world and bless the world.

Thank you so much for the work you are doing to heal yourself and your family. Every effort you make matters. You have already done so much and I feel so overjoyed for you to have even more knowledge and options available to you. You will find the answers you are seeking–even if it's not on the timetable you wish. Keep breathing. You are doing amazing.

Made in United States
Troutdale, OR
09/27/2023

13242232R00136